The History of
SUB-SAHARAN AFRICA

a select bibliography
of books and reviews, 1945-1975

Bibliographies
and
Guides
in
African Studies

James C. Armstrong
Editor

The History of
SUB-SAHARAN AFRICA

*a select bibliography
of books and reviews, 1945-1975*

WILLIAM E. MARTELLO

JEFFREY E. BUTLER

G.K.HALL &CO.

70 LINCOLN STREET, BOSTON, MASS.

Library of Congress Cataloging in Publication Data
Martello, William E
  The history of Sub-Saharan Africa.

  (Bibliographies and guides in African studies)
  Includes indexes.
  1. Africa, Sub-Saharan — History — Book reviews —
Indexes. 2. Africa, Sub-Saharan — History — Periodicals —
Indexes   I. Butler, Jeffrey, joint author.   II. Title.
III. Series.
Z3508.H5M37   [DT352.5]   967'.016   78-666
ISBN 0-8161-8002-4

This publication is printed on permanent/durable acid-free paper
MANUFACTURED IN THE UNITED STATES OF AMERICA

Contents

Preface

Since the end of World War Two the field of African studies has witnessed enormous growth. Accompanying this growth has been a proliferation of written material. The purpose of this Index is to present, in an organized fashion, information concerning one genre of written material--the book review. The Index provides a comprehensive listing of book reviews from eighteen select journals, encompassing the period 1945-1975. As far as possible, complete information is given for each review: the journal name, volume number, issue number, year, inclusive pagination, and reviewer.

We have chosen 560 books to include in this Index using the following selection criteria. The books listed are, for the most part, monographs. We have also included some edited collections which seem particularly important and influential. Moreover, these selections are largely restricted to the field of African history. Beyond this framework, selections were made on the basis of personal judgment and consultation with other Africanists. As a result, we have probably omitted some important works, while including lesser ones. On this account the final praise or blame rests with us.

Though this Index may seem to duplicate work done by David Henige in his Works in African History: An Index to Reviews, 1960-1974 (Waltham, MA: African Studies Association, 1976), it differs in some important respects. While we index far fewer journals than Henige, we provide more thorough coverage of those journals we do index. We also provide more complete information. Our book selection also differs from Henige's to a significant extent. Finally, we have provided both an author/title and a reviewer index, while Henige left his work unindexed. Still, the Henige index provides much useful information. If an individual uses his index in conjunction with ours, we believe that he can expect a far-ranging coverage of the field.

An index such as ours is constantly in need of updating and revision, especially in light of the wealth of currently-published monographs and reviews. We would thus strongly encourage others to expand our work to increase its utility to the student or scholar of African history.

Finally, we must extend our thanks to those whose time and judgment are reflected in this work. First and foremost, our thanks go to Richard Elphick, Associate Professor of History at Wesleyan University, whose advice and encouragement helped this Index to become more than it might otherwise have been; to Jim Armstrong, whose early contributions helped lift our project off the ground; to Peter Duignan, David Robinson, Robert Rotberg, Leonard Thompson, Douglas Wheeler, and Marcia Wright, whose contributions helped us to clarify in our own minds what we were intending to do in this Index; to Ann Crescimanno, Louise Fosa, and Dorothy Hay for providing early help, supplies, and sympathy; to Mary Rindfleisch, who performed much of the arduous task of journal-scanning with great accuracy; to Emily and Irene, for their patience during the final preparation of this work; and to Diane Mac Lean, who helped perform the final typing and proofreading duties with great diligence, accuracy, and humor.

Journals Indexed

Africa, v. 15-45 (1945-1975)

African Affairs, v. 44-74 (1945-1975)

African Historical Studies, v. 1-4 (1968-1971); succeeded by the
    International Journal of African Historical Studies

African Social Research, no. 1-20 (1966-1975); succeeds the Rhodes-
    Livingstone Journal

African Studies, v. 4-34 (1945-1975)

African Studies Bulletin/African Studies Review, v. 1-18 (1958-1975)

American Historical Review, v. 50-80 (1944/45-1975)

Bulletin-School of Oriental and African Studies, v. 11-38 (1943/46-
    1975)

Comparative Studies in Society and History, v. 1-17 (1958/59-1975)

English Historical Review, v. 60-90 (1945-1975)

Cambridge Historical Journal/Historical Journal, v. 8-13 (1944/46-
    1957), v. 1-18 (1958-1975)

History, v. 30-60 (1945-1975)

International Journal of African Historical Studies, v. 5-8 (1972-
    1975); succeeds African Historical Studies

Journal of African History, v. 1-16 (1960-1975)

Journal of Modern African Studies, v. 1-13 (1963-1975)

Race/Race and Class, v. 1-15 (1959/60-1973/74), v. 16 (1974/75)

Rhodes-Livingstone Journal, no. 3-38 (1945-1965); succeeded by African
    Social Research

Round Table, no. 138-260 (1945-1975)

Journal Abbreviations

Afr	Africa
Af Af	African Affairs
Af HS	African Historical Studies (succeeded by the International Journal of African Historical Studies)
Af SR	African Social Research
Af St	African Studies
Af StR	African Studies Bulletin/African Studies Review
AHR	American Historical Review
BSOAS	Bulletin-School of Oriental and African Studies
CSSH	Comparative Studies in Society and History
EHR	English Historical Review
HJC/HJ	Cambridge Historical Journal/Historical Journal
Hist	History
IJAHS	International Journal of African Historical Studies
JAH	Journal of African History
JMAS	Journal of Modern African Studies
Race	Race/Race and Class
RLJ	Rhodes-Livingstone Journal (succeeded by African Social Research)
RT	Round Table

Key to Entries

Author (individual or corporate), title, and publishing data were taken, wherever possible, from the Library of Congress cataloguing entries for these works, as cited in the National Union Catalog.

Review data is listed in the following order:

JOURNAL NAME (abbreviation)	VOLUME (if any)	NUMBER	YEAR	PAGINATION	REVIEWER'S NAME

example:

| Afr | 40 | 3 | 1970 | 283-4 | Richard Hill |

The History of Sub-Saharan Africa

a select bibliography of books and reviews, 1945-1975

1   'Abd al-Rahim, Muddathir
    IMPERIALISM AND NATIONALISM IN THE SUDAN, A STUDY IN CONSTITU-
    TIONAL AND POLITICAL DEVELOPMENT, 1899-1956.
    Oxford, Clarendon Press, 1969.

Afr	40	3	1970	283-4	Richard Hill
Af Af	70	279	1971	182-3	Ruth First
BSOAS	34	1	1971	150-1	G. N. Sanderson
JAH	11	2	1970	288-90	Robert O. Collins

2   Abir, Mordechai
    ETHIOPIA: THE ERA OF THE PRINCES: THE CHALLENGE OF ISLAM AND
    THE RE-UNIFICATION OF THE CHRISTIAN EMPIRE, 1769-1855.
    Harlow, Longmans, 1968.
    New York, Praeger, 1968.

Afr	41	1	1971	67	Virginia Luling
Af Af	71	285	1972	456-7	C. F. Beckingham
Af HS	3	1	1970	183-5	Harold G. Marcus
AHR	75	5	1969/70	1502-3	Robert L. Hess
BSOAS	33	2	1970	388-9	A. K. Irvine
Hist	55	184	1970	316	Kenneth Ingham
JAH	11	2	1970	280-2	Donald Crummey

3   Abun-Nasr, Jamil M.
    THE TIJANIYYA, A SUFI ORDER IN THE MODERN WORLD.
    London, New York, Oxford University Press, 1965.

Afr	37	3	1967	356-7	I. M. Lewis
BSOAS	30	1	1967	230-2	Humphrey J. Fisher
JMAS	8	3	1970	494-5	Charles O. Cecil

4   Adam, Heribert
    MODERNIZING RACIAL DOMINATION; SOUTH AFRICA'S POLITICAL DYNA-
    MICS.
    Berkeley, University of California Press, 1971.

Adeleye, R. A.

(Adam, Heribert)

Af SR	--	16	1973	508-9	Ray Simons
Af StR	14	2	1971	341-3	Christian P. Potholm
IJAHS	5	3	1972	479-84	Jeffrey Butler
JMAS	12	1	1974	137-41	Lawrence Frank

5   Adeleye, R. A.
POWER AND DIPLOMACY IN NORTHERN NIGERIA, 1804-1906: THE SOKOTO
CALIPHATE AND ITS ENEMIES.
London, Longman, 1971.
New York, Humanities Press, 1971.

Afr	42	4	1972	353	Murray Last
Af Af	72	286	1973	84-5	David E. Allyn
AHR	79	4	1974	1228-9	Daniel F. McCall
BSOAS	35	3	1972	675-6	Mervyn Hiskett
IJAHS	5	1	1972	142-4	Anthony Kirk-Greene
JAH	13	2	1972	332-5	Humphrey J. Fisher

6   Adiko, Assoi
HISTOIRE DES PEUPLES NOIRS. AVEC LA COLLABORATION D' ANDRÉ
CLÉRICI. COURS MOYEN.
Abidjan, C.E.D.A., 1961.

JMAS	2	1	1964	147-8	Godfrey N. Brown

7   Afigbo, Adiele Eberechukwu
THE WARRANT CHIEFS: INDIRECT RULE IN SOUTHEASTERN NIGERIA,
1891-1929.
London, Longman, 1972.

BSOAS	36	3	1973	725-7	A. H. M. Kirk-Greene
IJAHS	6	4	1973	716-8	G. I. Jones
JAH	14	3	1973	512-4	John D. Hargreaves
JMAS	11	3	1973	487-9	Samuel O. Okafor

8   AFRICA AND ITS EXPLORERS; MOTIVES, METHODS, AND IMPACT.
EDITED BY ROBERT I. ROTBERG.
Cambridge, Harvard University Press, 1970.

Af HS	4	2	1971	423-5	Hubert Deschamps
AHR	77	3	1972	813-4	John P. Halstead
BSOAS	35	1	1972	210	Michael Twaddle
Hist	57	189	1972	152	Kenneth Ingham

Ajayi, J. F. Ade

(AFRICA AND ITS EXPLORERS)
JMAS   9   4   1971   649-50   Lenwood G. Davis
Race   13   3   1971/72   381-2   Christopher Fyfe

9   AFRICAN PERSPECTIVES; PAPERS IN THE HISTORY, POLITICS AND ECO-
     NOMICS OF AFRICA PRESENTED TO THOMAS HODGKIN.
     EDITED BY CHRISTOPHER ALLEN AND R. W. JOHNSON.
     Cambridge, University Press, 1970.

     Af Af   70   281   1971   404-5   George Shepperson
     JAH   12   4   1971   653-5   Humphrey J. Fisher
     JMAS   9   3   1971   471-4   Richard L. Sklar
     Race   13   1   1971/72   116-7   Christopher Fyfe

10   AFRICAN SOCIETIES IN SOUTHERN AFRICA: HISTORICAL STUDIES.
     EDITED BY LEONARD THOMPSON.
     London, Heinemann, 1969.
     New York, Praeger, 1969.

     Af Af   69   275   1970   194-5   C. C. Saunders
     Af HS   3   2   1970   467-8   Richard B. Ford
     AHR   77   3   1972   822-3   Jeffrey Butler
     BSOAS   34   2   1971   449-50   Richard Gray
     Race   12   3   1970/71   371-3   Eva L. R. Meyerowitz

11   Agbodeka, Francis
     AFRICAN POLITICS AND BRITISH POLICY IN THE GOLD COAST, 1868-
     1900: A STUDY IN THE FORMS AND FORCE OF PROTEST.
     London, Longman, Evanston, Ill., Northwestern University Press,
     1971.

     Afr   43   2   1973   173-4   A. F. Robertson
     Af Af   72   286   1973   82-3   Edward Reynolds
     IJAHS   7   1   1974   169-72   R. E. Dumett
     JAH   13   3   1972   516-8   R. C. C. Law

12   Ajayi, J. F. Ade
     CHRISTIAN MISSIONS IN NIGERIA, 1841-1891; THE MAKING OF A NEW
     ÉLITE.
     Evanston, Ill., Northwestern University Press, 1965.

     Af Af   65   260   1966   264-5   Geoffrey Parrinder
     EHR   82   322   1967   192-3   John D. Hargreaves
     JAH   7   2   1966   348-9   Richard Gray
     Race   7   2   1965/66   209-10   Colin Newbury

Ajayi, J. F. Ade

13   Ajayi, J. F. Ade
     HISTORY OF WEST AFRICA; EDITED BY J. F. A. AJAYI AND MICHAEL
     CROWDER.
     London, Longman, 1971-1974.
     New York, Columbia University Press, 1972-1974.

     Vol. 1

Afr	43	4	1973	370-1	Robert Smith
Af Af	73	291	1974	235	D. H. Jones
AHR	80	5	1975	1372	Robert W. July
Hist	58	193	1973	324	Christopher Fyfe
IJAHS	6	1	1973	163-9	Yves Person
JAH	14	1	1973	129-38	J. D. Fage

     Vol. 2

Afr	45	3	1975	333	Robert Smith
Af Af	73	293	1974	486-7	D. H. Jones
IJAHS	8	2	1975	306-9	Martin A. Klein

14   Ajayi, J. F. Ade
     YORUBA WARFARE IN THE NINETEENTH CENTURY, BY J. F. A. AJAYI
     AND ROBERT SMITH.
     Cambridge, University Press, 1964.

Afr	43	1	1973	87	William Gutteridge
Af Af	64	257	1965	307-8	R. S. G. Stokes
Af Af	72	286	1973	76-9	R. C. C. Law
AHR	70	4	1964/65	1215	Philip D. Curtin
EHR	81	319	1966	413	George Shepperson
IJAHS	6	4	1973	695-700	Spencer H. Brown
JAH	6	3	1965	430-2	D. H. Jones
JMAS	13	3	1975	469-81	G. N. Uzoigwe

15   Akinjogbin, I. A.
     DAHOMEY AND ITS NEIGHBOURS, 1708-1818.
     Cambridge, Cambridge U.P., 1967.

Afr	39	2	1969	202-3	W. J. Argyle
Af HS	1	2	1968	298-300	Louis Brenner
AHR	74	1	1968/69	245-6	Graham Irwin
BSOAS	32	1	1969	213-4	Richard Gray
Hist	54	182	1969	463-4	David Birmingham
JAH	10	1	1969	179-81	J. D. Fage

Anderson, John E.

16   Akintoye, Stephen Adebanji
      REVOLUTION AND POWER POLITICS IN YORUBALAND, 1840-1893:
      IBADAN EXPANSION AND THE RISE OF EKITIPARAPO.
      London, Longman, 1971.
      New York, Humanities Press, 1971.

      Afr   42   1   1972   69-70   Robert Smith
      Af Af   72   286 1973   76-9   R. C. C. Law
      AHR   77   3   1972   818   Jean Herskovits
      BSOAS   36   3   1973   753   R. J. A. R. Rathbone
      IJAHS   5   3   1972   509-12   Earl H. Phillips
      JAH   14   1   1973   146   Robert Smith

17   Alagoa, Ebiergberi Joe
      THE SMALL BRAVE CITY-STATE; A HISTORY OF NEMBE-BRASS IN THE
      NIGER DELTA.
      Ibadan, Nigeria, Ibadan University Press, Madison, University
      of Wisconsin Press, 1964.

      Afr   36   3   1966   339-40   G. I. Jones
      Af Af   64   254 1965   63   -----
      Af St   24   2   1965   124-6   M. D. W. Jeffreys
      AHR   70   3   1964/65   880-1   Robert O. Collins
      JAH   6   2   1965   248   J. E. Flint

18   Ali, Abbas Ibrahim Muhammad
      THE BRITISH, THE SLAVE TRADE AND SLAVERY IN THE SUDAN, 1820-
      1881.
      Khartoum, Khartoum University Press, 1972.

      BSOAS   37   2   1974   513-4   Humphrey J. Fisher
      IJAHS   8   2   1975   288-90   Jay Spaulding
      JAH   15   3   1974   497-8   Richard Gray

19   Anderson, John E.
      THE STRUGGLE FOR THE SCHOOL: THE INTERACTION OF MISSIONARY,
      COLONIAL GOVERNMENT AND NATIONALIST ENTERPRISE IN THE DEVELOP-
      MENT OF FORMAL EDUCATION IN KENYA.
      London, Longman, 1970.

      JMAS   9   3   1971   493-5   Roger Van Zwanenberg

Anene, Joseph C.

20   Anene, Joseph C.
      SOUTHERN NIGERIA IN TRANSITION, 1885-1906; THEORY AND PRACTICE
      IN A COLONIAL PROTECTORATE.
      Cambridge, Cambridge U.P., 1966.

      Afr   36   4   1966   451-2   A. G. Hopkins
      Af Af   66   262   1967   82   -----
      AHR   72   2   1966/67   657-8   Henry S. Wilson
      BSOAS   29   3   1966   665-6   D. H. Jones
      JAH   7   3   1966   527-8   J. E. Flint

21   Ansprenger, Franz
      POLITIK IM SCHWARZEN AFRIKA; DIE MODERNEN POLITISCHEN BEWEGUN-
      GEN IM AFRIKA FRANZÖSISCHER PRÄGUNG.
      Köln, Westdeutscher Verlag, 1961.

      JAH   3   1   1962   152-4   S. K. Panter-Brick

22   Anstey, Roger
      BRITAIN AND THE CONGO IN THE NINETEENTH CENTURY.
      Oxford, Clarendon Press, 1962.

      AHR   70   1   1964/65   234   J. D. Fage
      BSOAS   26   2   1963   471-2   Marie de Kiewiet Hemphill
      EHR   79   313   1964   870   J. D. Hargreaves
      Hist   48   164   1963   414   A. J. Hanna
      JAH   5   2   1964   304-8   Jean Stengers

23   Anstey, Roger
      KING LEOPOLD'S LEGACY: THE CONGO UNDER BELGIAN RULE, 1908-
      1960.
      London, Oxford U.P., issued under the auspices of the Institute
      of Race Relations, 1966.

      Afr   37   1   1967   105-7   René Lemarchand
      Af Af   65   261   1966   356-7   J. P. Murray
      AHR   72   2   1966/67   660-1   Crawford Young
      EHR   82   324   1967   634   John D. Hargreaves
      Hist   54   180   1969   147   A. J. Hanna
      JAH   8   1   1967   171-2   Ruth Slade
      Race   8   2   1966/67   201-2   Mary Douglas

24   Apter, David Ernest
      GHANA IN TRANSITION; REV. ED.
      New York, Atheneum, 1963.

(Apter, David Ernest)
THE GOLD COAST IN TRANSITION.
Princeton, Princeton University Press, 1955.

Afr	26	3	1956	305-6	W. E. F. Ward
Af Af	55	220	1956	230-1	T. O. Elias
JMAS	4	3	1966	349-57	Robert L. Tignor
JMAS	7	1	1969	107-30	Jon Kraus

25   Apter, David Ernest
THE POLITICAL KINGDOM IN UGANDA; A STUDY IN BUREAUCRATIC
NATIONALISM.
Princeton, Princeton University Press, 1961.

Afr	32	3	1962	292	Lucy Mair
Af Af	61	243	1962	163-4	Nelson Mustoe
AHR	67	2	1961/62	494-5	Philip D. Curtin
JAH	3	1	1962	150-2	Kenneth Ingham
JMAS	4	3	1966	349-57	Robert L. Tignor

26   Argyle, William Johnson
THE FON OF DAHOMEY; A HISTORY AND ETHNOGRAPHY OF THE OLD
KINGDOM.
Oxford, Clarendon Press, 1966.

Afr	37	3	1967	369-60	J. Lombard
BSOAS	31	3	1968	655-7	D. H. Jones

27   Arkell, Anthony John
A HISTORY OF THE SUDAN: FROM THE EARLIEST TIMES IN 1821. WITH
A FOREWORD BY SIR HAROLD MAC MICHAEL.
London, University of London, Athlone Press, 1955.

Af Af	54	216	1955	231-2	Stewart Symes
AHR	61	1	1955/56	197	Garland G. Parker
EHR	70	277	1955	623-5	J. W. Crowfoot

28   Asiegbu, Johnson U. J.
SLAVERY AND THE POLITICS OF LIBERATION, 1787-1861: A STUDY OF
LIBERATED AFRICAN EMIGRATION AND BRITISH ANTI-SLAVERY POLICY.
Harlow, London, Longman, 1969.
New York, Africana Pub. Corp., 1969.

Afr	41	2	1971	177-8	Hubert Deschamps
Af Af	71	282	1972	90-1	P. E. H. Hair

ASPECTS OF CENTRAL AFRICAN HISTORY

(Asiegbu, Johnson U. J.)					
Af HS	4	1	1971	213-4	Johannes Postma
Af StR	14	3	1971	489-90	Martin A. Klein
AHR	76	2	1971	536-7	J. F. Ade Ajayi
BSOAS	34	1	1971	188-90	Humphrey J. Fisher
EHR	87	343	1972	431	Christopher Fyfe
JAH	12	2	1971	333-4	Roger Anstey

29   ASPECTS OF CENTRAL AFRICAN HISTORY.
EDITED BY T. O. RANGER.
Evanston, Ill., Northwestern University Press, 1968.
London, Ibadan, etc., Heinemann Educational, 1968.

Afr	44	2	1974	219-20	George Shepperson
Af HS	1	2	1968	302-9	L. H. Gann
Af SR	--	10	1970	796-9	H. W. Langworthy
AHR	74	5	1968/69	1680-1	Jean Herskovits
JAH	10	1	1969	178-9	J. R. Gray

30   ASPECTS OF WEST AFRICAN ISLAM.
EDITED BY DANIEL F. MC CALL AND NORMAN R. BENNETT.
Boston, African Studies Center, Boston University, 1971.

Afr	43	3	1973	274-5	Humphrey J. Fisher
AHR	80	5	1975	1372-3	Phyllis Ferguson
IJAHS	5	1	1972	125-9	David Robinson

31   Atanda, Joseph Adebowale
THE NEW OYO EMPIRE: INDIRECT RULE AND CHANGE IN WESTERN
NIGERIA, 1894-1934.
London, Longman, 1973.

Afr	45	1	1975	101	Robert Smith
BSOAS	37	2	1974	517-8	David Craig Dorward
JAH	15	2	1974	330-2	R. C. C. Law

32   Austen, Ralph A.
NORTHWEST TANZANIA UNDER GERMAN AND BRITISH RULE; COLONIAL
POLICY AND TRIBAL POLITICS, 1889-1939.
New Haven, Yale University Press, 1968.

Afr	41	2	1971	169-70	R. G. Abrahams
Af HS	2	2	1969	363-5	Israel Katoke, C. F. Holmes
AHR	75	7	1969/70	2103	Robert I. Rotberg

(Austen, Ralph A.)
BSOAS	32	3	1969	657-8	Andrew D. Roberts
Hist	57	189	1972	156-7	G. N. Sanderson
JAH	10	2	1969	332-3	Roland Oliver

33   Austin, Dennis
BRITAIN AND SOUTH AFRICA.
London, issued under the auspices of the Royal Institute of
International Affairs, Oxford University Press, 1966.

Af Af	66	263	1967	170-1	Kenneth Kirkwood
JAH	8	1	1967	173-4	Colin Legum
JMAS	4	4	1966	555-8	Franz Ansprenger
Race	8	3	1966/67	298-9	Christopher Fyfe

34   Austin, Dennis
POLITICS IN GHANA, 1946-1960.
Issued under the auspices of the Royal Institute of International Affairs, London, New York, Oxford University Press,
1964.

Af Af	64	255	1965	120	Joseph Kambu
Af HS	4	3	1971	714-6	A. A. Castagno
JAH	6	2	1965	243-5	B. D. G. Folson
JMAS	3	2	1965	301-4	Henry L. Bretton
JMAS	7	1	1969	107-30	Jon Kraus

35   Awolowo, Obafemi
AWO; THE AUTOBIOGRAPHY OF CHIEF OBAFEMI AWOLOWO.
Cambridge, University Press, 1960.

Af Af	60	241	1961	542-3	-----
JMAS	1	1	1963	122-5	David Williams

36   Axelson, Eric Victor
PORTUGAL AND THE SCRAMBLE FOR AFRICA, 1875-1891.
Johannesburg, Witwatersrand University Press, 1967.

Af Af	68	271	1969	173-4	M. Katzen
AHR	73	4	1967/68	1102-3	J. Duffy
HJ	13	3	1970	562-4	A. S. Kanya-Forstner
JAH	9	2	1968	335-6	Roland Oliver
JMAS	7	3	1969	544-6	Edward A. Alpers

Axelson, Eric Victor

37   Axelson, Eric Victor
     PORTUGUESE IN SOUTH-EAST AFRICA, 1600-1700.
     Johannesburg, Witwatersrand University Press, 1960.

     Afr   32   2   1962   181-2   A. H. J. Prins
     AHR   66   4   1960/61   1110-1   Virginia Rau
     EHR   77   303   1962   370-1   C. R. Boxer
     Hist   46   157   1961   177-8   C. R. Boxer
     JAH   2   2   1961   328-9   Roland Oliver

38   Ayandele, Emmanuel Ayankanmi
     HOLY JOHNSON, PIONEER OF AFRICAN NATIONALISM, 1836-1917.
     London, Cass, 1970.
     New York, Humanities Press, 1970.

     Afr   42   1   1972   71-2   A. H. M. Kirk-Greene
     Af Af   71   283   1972   209-10   Jonathan Derrick
     AHR   77   3   1972   817   Robert Heussler
     BSOAS   34   3   1971   660-2   Humphrey J. Fisher
     IJAHS   5   3   1972   509-12   Earl H. Phillips
     JAH   13   1   1972   165-8   P. Olisanwuche Esedebe

39   Ayandele, Emmanuel Ayankanmi
     THE MISSIONARY IMPACT ON MODERN NIGERIA, 1842-1919: A POLITI-
     CAL AND SOCIAL ANALYSIS.
     London, Longmans, 1966.
     New York, Humanities Press, 1967.

     JAH   9   1   1968   176-7   J. R. Gray

40   Azikiwe, Nmandi
     MY ODYSSEY: AN AUTOBIOGRAPHY.
     London, C. Hurst, 1970.
     New York, Praeger, 1970.

     Afr   42   1   1972   71-2   A. H. M. Kirk-Greene
     IJAHS   5   2   1972   352-4   Donald Rothchild
     JMAS   10   2   1972   323-4   Naomi Mitchison

41   Bâ, Amadou Hampaté
     L'EMPIRE PEUL DU MACINA, PAR A. H. BA ET J. DAGET.
     Paris, Mouton, 1962- .

     L'EMPIRE PEUL DU MACINA, PAR AMADOU HAMPATE BA ET JACQUES
     DAGET. ÉTUDES SOUDANAISES, NO. 3.

Ballinger, Margaret

(Bâ, Amadou Hampaté)
Kolouba, Institut Français d'Afrique Noire, Centre du Soudan, 1955.

Vol. 1: 1818-1853
Afr   30 1   1960   86   D. W. Arnott

42   Baer, George W.
     THE COMING OF THE ITALIAN-ETHIOPIAN WAR.
     Cambridge, Harvard University Press, 1967.

     AHR   73 3   1967/68 856   M. Salvadori

43   Baëta, C. G.
     PROPHETISM IN GHANA, A STUDY OF SOME "SPIRITUAL" CHURCHES.
     London, SCM Press, 1962.

     BSOAS   27 1   1964   238   F. G. B.
     JMAS   1 2   1963   278-9   E. Dammann

44   Balandier, Georges
     LA VIE QUOTIDIENNE AU ROYAUME DE KONGO DU XVIe AU XVIIIe
     SIÈCLE.
     Paris, Hachette, 1965.

     DAILY LIFE IN THE KINGDOM OF THE KONGO: FROM THE SIXTEENTH TO
     THE EIGHTEENTH CENTURY; TRANSLATED FROM THE FRENCH BY HELEN
     WEAVER.
     London, Allen and Unwin, 1968.
     New York, Pantheon Books, 1968.

     Afr   39 1   1969   62-8   J. Vansina
     Af Af   68 270   1969   64-5   Donal Cruise O'Brien
     BSOAS   31 3   1968   655   Richard Gray
     JAH   9 2   1968   332   David Birmingham

45   Ballinger, Margaret
     FROM UNION TO APARTHEID; A TREK TO ISOLATION.
     Cape Town, Juta, 1969.
     Folkestone, Bailey Bros. and Swinfen, 1969.
     New York, Praeger, 1969.

     Af Af   69 277   1970   408-9   Kenneth Kirkwood
     Af HS   3 2   1970   503-6   Laurence Salomon

Barber, James P.

(Ballinger, Margaret)					
Af St	29	4	1970	305-6	Julius Lewin
Af StR	14	1	1971	159-61	Richard David Ralston
AHR	75	6	1969/70	1758-60	Leonard Thompson
JAH	12	1	1971	164-5	Christopher R. Hill
Race	12	1	1970/71	118-20	Adrian Leftwich

46 Barber, James P.
IMPERIAL FRONTIER: A STUDY OF RELATIONS BETWEEN THE BRITISH
AND THE PASTORAL TRIBES OF NORTH EAST UGANDA.
Nairobi, East African Pub. House, 1968.

Af HS	2	2	1969	343-4	John Tosh
Hist	57	189	1972	156-7	G. N. Sanderson
JAH	10	3	1969	501-3	J. E. Lamphear
JMAS	9	3	1971	487-90	Maina Kagombe
Race	11	3	1969/70	383-4	Michael Twaddle

47 Barber, James P.
RHODESIA: THE ROAD TO REBELLION
London, New York, pub. for the Institute of Race Relations by
Oxford U.P., 1967.

Af Af	69	277	1970	406-8	Kenneth Kirkwood
Race	9	3	1967/68	386-8	Christopher Fyfe

48 Barber, James P.
SOUTH AFRICA'S FOREIGN POLICY, 1945-1970.
London, New York, Oxford University Press, 1973.

Af Af	74	294	1975	106-7	Margaret Doxey
Af StR	17	1	1974	280-2	Timothy M. Shaw
JAH	15	3	1974	524	J. E. Spence
JMAS	12	4	1974	703-5	C. W. de Kiewiet

49 Barnes, John Arundel
POLITICS IN A CHANGING SOCIETY; A POLITICAL HISTORY OF THE
FORT JAMESON NGONI
Cape Town, New York, published for the Rhodes-Livingstone In-
stitute by Oxford University Press, 1954.
Manchester, published for the Institute for Social Research,
University of Zambia, by Manchester University Press, 1967.

Afr	25	2	1955	197-8	Margaret Read
Af St	14	3	1955	138-9	Philip Mayer

(Barnes, John Arundel)
<u>2d edition</u>
JMAS   6   2   1968   282-4   John McCracken

50   Barry, Boubacar
LE ROYAUME DU WAALO; LE SÉNÉGAL AVANT LA CONQUÊTE.
PREF. DE SAMIR AMIN.
Paris, F. Maspero, 1972.

IJAHS	6	4	1973	679-81	Philip Curtin
JAH	15	2	1974	326-8	Charlotte Quinn

51   Bascom, William Russell
CONTINUITY AND CHANGE IN AFRICAN CULTURES, EDITED BY WILLIAM R.
BASCOM AND MELVILLE J. HERSKOVITS.
Chicago, University of Chicago Press, 1959.

Afr	30	4	1960	406-7	J. Vansina
Af Af	61	245	1962	353-4	-----

52   Bascom, William Russell
THE YORUBA OF SOUTHWESTERN NIGERIA.
New York, Holt, Rinehart and Winston, 1969.

Afr	41	1	1971	66-7	Eva Gillies
Af SR	--	11	1971	76-8	Fola Soremekun
JAH	12	3	1971	499-501	Kola Folayan

53   Bauer, Pèter Tamàs
WEST AFRICAN TRADE: A STUDY OF COMPETITION, OLIGOPOLY AND
MONOPOLY IN A CHANGING ECONOMY.
Cambridge, University Press, 1954.

Afr	26	2	1956	196-9	P. Ady

54   Behrman, Lucy C.
MUSLIM BROTHERHOODS AND POLITICS IN SENEGAL.
Cambridge, Harvard University Press, 1970.

Af HS	4	1	1971	183-5	David Robinson
Af StR	14	2	1971	332-4	Robert A. Mortimer
JMAS	11	4	1973	675-81	Clement Cottingham

Bello, Sir Ahmadu

55   Bello, Sir Ahmadu
      MY LIFE.
      Cambridge, University Press, 1962.

Af Af	62	247	1963	168-9	Iain Gunn
JMAS	1	1	1963	122-5	David Williams

56   Bennett, George
      KENYA, A POLITICAL HISTORY: THE COLONIAL PERIOD.
      London, Oxford University Press, 1963 (i.e., 1964).

AHR	70	4	1964/65	1112-4	David E. Gardinier
EHR	80	317	1965	871	George Shepperson
JAH	5	2	1964	330-1	C. Gertzel
Race	6	1	1964/65	75-6	F. B. Welbourn

57   Bennett, George
      THE KENYATTA ELECTION: KENYA 1960-1961, BY GEORGE BENNETT AND
      CARL G. ROSBERG.
      London, New York, published on behalf of the Institute of Com-
      monwealth Studies, Oxford, by Oxford University Press, 1961.

Afr	32	3	1962	299	Lucy Mair
JAH	4	1	1963	148-50	Colin Leys
RLJ	--	31	1962	78-80	H. Noak

58   Benson, Mary
      THE AFRICAN PATRIOTS, THE STORY OF THE AFRICAN NATIONAL
      CONGRESS OF SOUTH AFRICA.
      London, Faber and Faber, 1963.
      Chicago, Encyclopedia Britannica Press, 1964 (c1963).

Af Af	63	250	1964	63	Nelson Mustoe
JAH	5	2	1964	329-30	Shula Marks
JMAS	1	4	1963	548-9	S. Trapido
Race	5	1	1963/64	96-7	Neville Rubin

59   Benson, Mary
      TSHEKIDI KHAMA.
      London, Faber and Faber, 1960.

JAH	2	2	1961	339-40	I. Schapera

60   Benzing, Brigitta
      DIE GESCHICHTE UND DAS HERRSCHAFTSSYSTEM DER DAGOMBA.
      Meisenheim am Glan, A. Hain, 1971.

      Afr   43 4   1973   375-6   Rüdiger Schott

61   Berger, Elena L.
      LABOUR, RACE, AND COLONIAL RULE: THE COPPERBELT FROM 1924 TO
      INDEPENDENCE.
      Oxford, Clarendon Press, 1974.

      IJAHS   8   3   1975   536-8   J. R. Hooker
      Race   16 3   1974/75   329-31   Basker Vashee

62   Beshir, Mohammed Omer
      EDUCATIONAL DEVELOPMENT IN THE SUDAN, 1898-1956.
      Oxford, Clarendon Press, 1969.

      Afr   40 3   1970   289-90   Richard Hill
      BSOAS   33 2   1970   446-7   P. M. H.
      JAH   11 1   1970   157-8   Lilian Sanderson
      JMAS   8   2   1970   334-6   Elizabeth Hodgkin

63   Beshir, Mohammed Omer
      THE SOUTHERN SUDAN: BACKGROUND TO CONFLICT.
      London, C. Hurst and Co., 1968.
      New York, F. A. Praeger, 1968.

      Afr   39 3   1969   308-9   Jean Buxton
      Af Af   68 270 1969   63-4   J. B. Richmond
      Af HS   2   1   1969   175-9   John Sommer
      AHR   74 3   1968/69   1058-9   Robert O. Collins
      Race   11 1   1969/70   91-4   Oliver Albino

64   Bienen, Henry
      KENYA: THE POLITICS OF PARTICIPATION AND CONTROL.
      Princeton, Princeton University Press, 1974.

      Afr   45 1   1975   105-6   Lucy Mair
      Af SR   -- 19   1975   764-5   Malcolm Wallis
      JAH   16 3   1975   476-7   John Lonsdale
      JMAS   12 4   1974   681-4   Edmond J. Keller

Bienen, Henry

65   Bienen, Henry
     TANZANIA; PARTY TRANSFORMATION AND ECONOMIC DEVELOPMENT.
     Princeton, Princeton University Press, 1967.

Af SR	--	6	1968	487-9	William Tordoff
IJAHS	7	3	1974	533-7	Jonathan Barker

66   Bing, Geoffrey
     REAP THE WHIRLWIND: AN ACCOUNT OF KWAME NKRUMAH'S GHANA FROM
     1950-1966.
     London, MacGibbon and Kee, 1968.

Af Af	69	275	1970	190-1	Richard Rathbone
JMAS	7	1	1969	107-30	Jon Kraus

67   Binns, C. T.
     THE LAST ZULU KING; THE LIFE AND DEATH OF CETSHWAYO.
     London, Longmans, 1963.

JAH	4	3	1963	467-8	Shula Marks

68   Biobaku, Saburi Oladeni
     THE EGBA AND THEIR NEIGHBOURS, 1842-1872.
     Oxford, Clarendon Press, 1957.

Afr	28	2	1958	172-3	G. I. Jones
BSOAS	21	3	1958	667-8	J. E. Flint
EHR	74	290	1959	177-8	Freda Wolfson
Hist	43	148	1958	160-2	George Shepperson

69   Birmingham, David
     THE PORTUGUESE CONQUEST OF ANGOLA.
     London, New York, Oxford University Press, 1965.

Afr	36	1	1966	99-100	A. C. Edwards
EHR	81	321	1966	841-2	T. Price
JAH	7	1	1966	162	Douglas L. Wheeler
Race	7	2	1965/66	209	Roger Anstey

70   Birmingham, David
     TRADE AND CONFLICT IN ANGOLA: THE MBUNDU AND THEIR NEIGHBOURS
     UNDER THE INFLUENCE OF THE PORTUGUESE, 1483-1790.
     Oxford, Clarendon Press, 1966.

Bohannan, Paul

(Birmingham, David)

Afr	37	3	1967	362-3	A. C. Edwards
Af Af	66	264	1967	277-8	Mabel Jackson Haight
AHR	72	3	1966/67	1049-50	Daniel F. McCall
BSOAS	30	3	1967	767	James Duffy
EHR	83	327	1968	388-9	C. R. Boxer
Hist	52	176	1967	378	C. R. Boxer
JAH	8	3	1967	546-8	Jan Vansina
Race	9	1	1967/68	110-2	Allen Isaacman

71 Bley, Helmut
KOLONIALHERRSCHAFT UND SOZIALSTRUKTUR IN DEUTSCH-SÜDWESTAFRIKA
1894-1914
Hamburg, Leibniz-Verlag, 1968.

SOUTH-WEST AFRICA UNDER GERMAN RULE; ENGLISH EDITION TRANSLATED
FROM THE GERMAN, EDITED AND PREPARED BY HUGH RIDLEY.
London, Heinemann, 1971.

SOUTH-WEST AFRICA UNDER GERMAN RULE, 1894-1914. ENGLISH ED.
TRANSLATED, EDITED, AND PREPARED BY HUGH RIDLEY.
Evanston, Northwestern University Press, 1971.

Af StR	15	2	1972	325-7	Richard Dale
AHR	74	2	1968/69	685-6	Lewis H. Gann
Hist	57	189	1972	157-8	Peter Hatton
IJAHS	6	1	1973	121-6	L. H. Gann
JAH	11	3	1970	459-61	Marcia Wright
JMAS	9	3	1971	484-6	Ibrahim A. Gambari

72 Boahen, A. Adu
BRITAIN, THE SAHARA, AND THE WESTERN SUDAN, 1788-1861.
Oxford, Clarendon Press, 1964.

Afr	35	2	1965	217-8	A. H. M. Kirk-Greene
Af Af	64	255	1965	130-1	Duncan Cumming
AHR	70	4	1964/65	1211-2	Margaret L. Bates
BSOAS	28	3	1965	670	M. Hiskett
EHR	80	316	1965	617-8	G. N. Sanderson
Hist	50	169	1965	268-9	John D. Hargreaves
JAH	6	1	1965	126-8	Henri Brunschwig

73 Bohannan, Paul
AFRICA AND AFRICANS.
Garden City, N. Y., published for the American Museum of
Natural History by the Natural History Press, 1964.

Bovill, E. W.

(Bohannan, Paul)
JAH 6 1 1965 120-3 Hubert Deschamps

AFRICA AND AFRICANS, BY PAUL BOHANNAN AND PHILIP CURTIN.
REV. ED.
Garden City, N. Y., published for the American Museum of
Natural History by the Natural History Press, 1971.

IJAHS 6 3 1973 493-4 C. F. Holmes

74 Bovill, E. W.
THE GOLDEN TRADE OF THE MOORS.
London, New York, Oxford University Press, 1958; 2d ed., 1968.

Afr	29	3	1959	306-8	J. D. Fage
Af Af	57	227	1958	158-9	E. A. Alport
AHR	64	2	1958/59	417-8	Sydney Nettleton Fisher
BSOAS	22	2	1959	395-6	D. H. Jones
EHR	74	291	1959	335-6	W. H. C. Frend
Hist	44	151	1959	146	Gervase Mathew

2d edition

Af Af	69	275	1968	198	David Birmingham
Af HS	2	1	1969	171-2	Louis Brenner
BSOAS	32	1	1969	215-6	D. H. Jones

75 Boxer, Charles Ralph
THE DUTCH SEABORNE EMPIRE, 1600-1800.
New York, Knopf, 1965.

AHR 73 3 1967/68 836-7 P. B. Cares

76 Boxer, Charles Ralph
FORT JESUS AND THE PORTUGUESE IN MOMBASA, 1593-1729, BY C. R.
BOXER AND CARLOS DE AZEVEDO.
London, Hollis and Carter, 1960.

EHR	76	301	1961	718	George Shepperson
Hist	45	155	1960	281-3	Roland Oliver
JAH	1	2	1960	321-3	G. S. P. Freeman-Grenville

77 Boxer, Charles Ralph
THE PORTUGUESE SEABORNE EMPIRE, 1415-1825.
London, Hutchinson, 1969.
New York, A. A. Knopf, 1969.

(Boxer, Charles Ralph)

Af StR	14	3	1971	505-7	Thomas H. Henriksen
AHR	75	6	1969/70	1692-4	Dauril Alden
BSOAS	34	1	1971	203	D. K. Bassett
EHR	86	341	1971	836-7	A. J. R. Russell-Wood
JAH	11	2	1970	279	David Birmingham
Race	12	3	1970/71	370-1	Douglas L. Wheeler

78   Boxer, Charles Ralph
PORTUGUESE SOCIETY IN THE TROPICS; THE MUNICIPAL COUNCILS OF
GOA, MACAO, BAHIA, AND LUANDA, 1510-1800.
Madison, University of Wisconsin Press, 1965.

BSOAS	29	2	1966	465	Hugh Tinker
EHR	82	323	1967	387-8	John Lynch
Hist	52	176	1967	376-7	K. G. Davies
JAH	7	2	1966	343-4	David Birmingham

79   Boxer, Charles Ralph
RACE RELATIONS IN THE PORTUGUESE COLONIAL EMPIRE, 1415-1825.
Oxford, Clarendon Press, 1963.

Af Af	63	253	1964	315	-----
AHR	69	4	1963/64	1135	Stanley G. Payne
Hist	51	171	1966	90-1	J. H. Parry
JAH	5	2	1964	324-5	David Birmingham
Race	5	3	1963/64	78-80	C. H. Green

80   Bradbury, R. E.
BENIN STUDIES.   EDITED, WITH AN INTRODUCTION BY PETER MORTON
WILLIAMS.   FOREWORD BY DARYLL FORDE.
London, New York, published for the International African In-
stitute by Oxford University Press, 1973.

Afr	44	3	1974	315-6	Lucy Mair
Af Af	73	293	1974	491	Robin Law

81   Brausch, Georges
BELGIAN ADMINISTRATION IN THE CONGO.
Issued under the auspices of the Institute of Race Relations,
London, New York, Oxford University Press, 1961.

Afr	32	4	1962	407-8	J. Vansina
Race	3	2	1961/62	84-5	H. J. Simons
RLJ	--	31	1962	72-4	C. M. N. White

Brenner, Louis

82   Brenner, Louis
      THE SHEHUS OF KUKAWA; A HISTORY OF THE AL-KANEMI DYNASTY OF
      BORNU.
      Oxford, Clarendon Press, 1973.

      Afr   44 2   1974   216   Murray Last
      AHR   80 5   1975   1373-4   Robert O. Collins
      BSOAS   36 3   1973   720-1   Humphrey J. Fisher
      IJAHS   7 1   1974   148-50   Mervyn Hiskett
      JAH   15 3   1974   501-3   Jay Spaulding

83   Brett, E. A.
      COLONIALISM AND UNDERDEVELOPMENT IN EAST AFRICA: THE POLITICS
      OF ECONOMIC CHANGE, 1919-1939.
      London, Heinemann, 1973.
      New York, NOK Publishers, 1973.

      Af Af   74 295 1975   230-1   C. C. Wrigley
      AHR   79 5   1974   1606-7   Ralph A. Austen
      IJAHS   8 1   1975   149-53   Nizar A. Motani

84   Bretton, Henry L.
      POWER AND STABILITY IN NIGERIA; THE POLITICS OF DECOLONIZATION.
      New York, F. A. Praeger, 1962.

      JMAS   1 2   1963   261-2   Douglas G. Anglin

85   Bretton, Henry L.
      THE RISE AND FALL OF KWAME NKRUMAH: A STUDY OF PERSONAL RULE
      IN AFRICA.
      London, Pall Mall Press, 1966.
      New York, Praeger, 1967 (c1966).

      Af Af   67 267 1968   169-70   Richard Rathbone
      JMAS   7 1   1969   107-30   Jon Kraus

86   BRITAIN AND GERMANY IN AFRICA: IMPERIAL RIVALRY AND COLONIAL
      RULE. EDITED BY PROSSER GIFFORD AND WILLIAM ROGER LOUIS. WITH
      THE ASSISTANCE OF ALISON SMITH.
      New Haven, Yale University Press, 1967.

      Af Af   67 269 1968   358-60   Marcia Wright
      Af SR   -- 8   1968   636   E. R. Turton
      Af St   31 1   1972   55-8   T. R. H. Davenport

Brunschwig, Henri

(BRITAIN AND GERMANY IN AFRICA:)

AHR	74	3	1968/69	948-9	Margaret L. Bates
BSOAS	33	1	1970	235-6	G. N. Sanderson
EHR	84	333	1969	816-7	A. J. P. Taylor
Hist	54	180	1969	148-9	R. C. Bridges
JAH	10	4	1969	684-7	Anthony Atmore
JMAS	7	3	1969	542-3	Fred L. Hadsel

87   Brookes, Edgar Harry
A HISTORY OF NATAL, BY EDGAR H. BROOKES AND COLIN DE B. WEBB.
Pietermaritzburg, University of Natal Press, 1965.

Af Af	68	270	1969	68-9	M. Katzen
Af HS	2	1	1969	167-70	Leslie Clement Duly
Af St	25	4	1966	233-5	B. M. Nicholls
AHR	72	1	1966/67	256-7	A. W. Rees
Hist	53	178	1968	298-9	Freda Harcourt
JAH	8	3	1967	529-40	Shula Marks

88   Brunschwig, Henri
L'AVÈNEMENT DE L'AFRIQUE NOIRE, DU XIXe SIÈCLE À NOS JOURS.
Paris, Libraire A. Colin, 1963.

AHR	69	2	1963/64	531-2	Norman R. Bennett
JAH	5	1	1964	133-4	Roland Oliver

89   Brunschwig, Henri
L'EXPANSION ALLEMANDE OUTRE-MER DU XVe SIÈCLE À NOS JOURS.
Paris, Presses Universitaires de France, 1957.

AHR	64	2	1958/59	442	Harry R. Rudin
EHR	73	289	1958	710-1	W. P. Morrell
Hist	45	155	1960	284-5	H. G. Pitt

90   Brunschwig, Henri
MYTHES ET RÉALITÉS DE L'IMPÉRIALISME COLONIAL FRANÇAIS, 1871-
1914.
Paris, A. Colin, 1960.

FRENCH COLONIALISM, 1871-1914: MYTHS AND REALITIES.
ENGLISH TRANSLATION BY WILLIAM GRANVILLE BROWN, INTRODUCTION
BY RONALD E. ROBINSON.
London, Pall Mall Press, 1964, 1966.
New York, Praeger, 1966 (c1964).

Buell, Raymond Leslie

(Brunschwig, Henri)

Af HS	1	1	1968	137-9	William B. Cohen
AHR	66	2	1960/61	446-7	John F. Cady
Hist	54	180	1969	147-8	A. J. Hanna
JAH	2	1	1961	158-60	Ronald Robinson
JAH	7	3	1966	524-5	Colin Newbury
JMAS	6	3	1968	451-3	Paul Semonin

91   Buell, Raymond Leslie
     ... LIBERIA: A CENTURY OF SURVIVAL, 1847-1947.
     Philadelphia, University of Pennsylvania Press, the University
     Museum, 1947.

Afr	17	4	1947	295	L. P. Mair

92   Buijtenhuijs, Robert
     LE MOUVEMENT 'MAU-MAU'. UNE RÉVOLTE PAYSANNE ET ANTICOLONIALE
     EN AFRIQUE NOIRE.
     La Haye, Mouton, 1971.

Afr	43	4	1973	374-5	Bernardo Bernardi
JAH	14	1	1973	170-1	Frank Furedi

93   Busia, Kofi Abrefa
     AFRICA IN SEARCH OF DEMOCRACY.
     London, Routledge and K. Paul, 1967.
     New York, Praeger, 1967.

Af Af	68	271	1969	177	Richard Rathbone
JMAS	8	2	1970	329-31	Christian P. Potholm

94   Busia, Kofi Abrefa
     THE POSITION OF THE CHIEF IN THE MODERN POLITICAL SYSTEM OF
     ASHANTI; A STUDY OF THE INFLUENCE OF CONTEMPORARY SOCIAL
     CHANGES ON ASHANTI POLITICAL INSTITUTIONS.
     London, New York, published for the International African In-
     stitute, by the Oxford University Press, 1951.

Afr	22	2	1952	178-9	G. Saunders
Af Af	68	270	1969	72	Richard Rathbone
Af St	18	2	1959	88-90	M. D. W. Jeffreys

95   Butler, Jeffrey
       THE LIBERAL PARTY AND THE JAMESON RAID.
       Oxford, Clarendon Press, 1968.

Af Af	68	272	1969	277-8	T. R. H. Davenport
Af HS	3	1	1970	192-3	Robin W. Winks
Af St	29	2	1970	149-50	A. J. Dachs
BSOAS	32	2	1969	465-6	Anthony Atmore
EHR	84	333	1969	872-3	J. R. Vincent
Hist	54	182	1969	438	R. T. Shannon

96   Cairns, H. Alan C.
       PRELUDE TO IMPERIALISM; BRITISH REACTIONS TO CENTRAL AFRICAN
       SOCIETY, 1840-1890
       London, Routledge and K. Paul, 1965.

Afr	36	3	1966	329-30	A. C. Ross
EHR	82	323	1967	431-2	George Shepperson
JAH	8	1	1967	167-7	Roger Anstey
Race	8	2	1966/67	195-6	Christopher Fyfe

97   THE CAMBRIDGE HISTORY OF ISLAM; EDITED BY P. M. HOLT, ANN K. S.
       LAMBTON AND BERNARD LEWIS.
       Cambridge, University Press, 1970.

AHR	77	1	1972	115-6	George Rentz
AHR	77	1	1972	116-7	Robert L. Tignor
BSOAS	35	2	1972	355-8	R. C. Ostle
EHR	87	343	1972	348-57	A. H. Hourani
Hist	57	189	1972	159-61	J. S. F. Parker
IJAHS	5	1	1972	140-1	Norman R. Bennett, Louis Brenner
JAH	12	3	1970	490-2	Roland Oliver

98   Caplan, Gerald L.
       THE ELITES OF BAROTSELAND, 1878-1969; A POLITICAL HISTORY OF
       ZAMBIA'S WESTERN PROVINCE.
       Berkeley, University of California Press, 1970.
       London, C. Hurst, 1970.

Af Af	71	283	1972	211-2	Q. N. Parsons
Af SR	--	13	1972	232-4	Robert H. Bates
Af StR	15	2	1972	329-30	Ed Steinhart
AHR	77	3	1972	821	Alan R. Booth
IJAHS	5	3	1972	512-4	Robert I. Rotberg

Carter, Gwendolen Margaret

    (Caplan, Gerald L.)
JAH	12	4	1971	655-7	Mutumba Mainga Bull
JMAS	11	2	1973	332-3	Helmuth Heisler

99   Carter, Gwendolen Margaret
    THE POLITICS OF INEQUALITY; SOUTH AFRICA SINCE 1948.
    New York, F. A. Praeger, 1958.

Afr	29	2	1959	200-4	Sheila Patterson
AHR	64	2	1958/59	337-8	Colin Rhys Lovell

100   Cartwright, John R.
    POLITICS IN SIERRA LEONE 1947-67.
    Toronto, University of Toronto Press, 1970.

Af Af	71	282	1972	91-2	Christopher Clapham
Af HS	4	2	1971	457-8	Christopher Fyfe
JMAS	9	2	1971	329-31	Robert E. Johnston

101   Cary, Joyce
    THE CASE FOR AFRICAN FREEDOM.
    London, Secker and Warburg, 1941.

Afr	16	1	1946	66	Edwin W. Smith

102   Castagno, Alphonso Anthony
    SOMALIA.
    New York, Carnegie Endowment for International Peace, 1959.

Afr	30	1	1960	93	I. M. Lewis
Af St	20	1	1961	92	I. M. Lewis

103   Cell, John Whitson
    BRITISH COLONIAL ADMINISTRATION IN THE MID-NINETEENTH CENTURY;
    THE POLICY-MAKING PROCESS.
    New Haven, Yale University Press, 1970.

EHR	86	338	1971	135-8	A. F. McC. Madden
HJ	15	3	1972	562-9	Ged Martin
Hist	57	189	1972	137-9	Donald Southgate
IJAHS	5	2	1972	289-91	Margaret L. Bates
JAH	11	4	1970	615-6	G. E. Metcalfe

104   Ceulemans, P.
      LA QUESTION ARABE ET LE CONGO, 1883–1892.
      Bruxelles, 1959.

      | Afr | 30 | 4 | 1960 | 414 | P. M. Holt |
      | JAH | 1 | 1 | 1960 | 166–8 | Alison Smith |

105   Chambers, Robert
      SETTLEMENT SCHEMES IN TROPICAL AFRICA: A STUDY OF ORGANIZA-
      TIONS AND DEVELOPMENT.
      London, Routledge and K. Paul, 1969.

      | Afr | 40 | 3 | 1970 | 290–1 | D. Paul Lumsden |
      | Af Af | 69 | 277 | 1970 | 397 | Gavin Green |
      | JMAS | 9 | 1 | 1971 | 143–6 | A. H. Hanson |

106   Chidzero, B. T. G.
      TANGANYIKA AND INTERNATIONAL TRUSTEESHIP.
      London, New York, Oxford University Press, 1961.

      | Af Af | 60 | 241 | 1961 | 541–2 | Iain Gunn |
      | Af Af | 61 | 242 | 1962 | 64–5 | Iain Gunn |
      | JAH | 4 | 1 | 1963 | 147–8 | Colin Leys |
      | Race | 3 | 1 | 1961/62 | 93–4 | Kenneth Ingham |
      | RLJ | -- | 30 | 1961 | 61–4 | Richard Brown |

107   Chilcote, Ronald H.
      PORTUGUESE AFRICA.
      Englewood Cliffs, N. J., Prentice-Hall, 1967.

      | Af Af | 67 | 266 | 1968 | 77–8 | Mabel Jackson Haight |
      | Af HS | 2 | 1 | 1969 | 152–3 | Thomas Okuma |
      | JMAS | 6 | 1 | 1968 | 115–6 | Walter Rodney |

108   Church, Ronald James Harrison
      WEST AFRICA; A STUDY OF THE ENVIRONMENT AND OF MAN'S USE OF IT.
      London, New York, Longmans, Green, 1957.

      | Afr | 28 | 2 | 1958 | 175–6 | R. Mansell Prothero |
      | Af Af | 66 | 264 | 1967 | 260–1 | N. C. Pollock |
      | JAH | 1 | 1 | 1960 | 184–5 | P. Alexandre |

Clark, John Desmond

109   Clark, John Desmond
      THE PREHISTORY OF SOUTHERN AFRICA.
      Harmondsworth, Middlesex, Penguin Books, 1959.

AHR	77	3	1972	812-3	Jan Vansina
JAH	2	1	1961	153-4	Bridget Allchin

110   Clegg, Edward Marshall
      RACE AND POLITICS; PARTNERSHIP IN THE FEDERATION OF RHODESIA
      AND NYASALAND.
      London, New York, Oxford University Press, 1960.

Afr	31	4	1961	383	G. Beresford-Stooke
Af Af	60	239	1961	192-3	M. L. Clark
AHR	66	3	1960/61	772	Paul Knaplund
JAH	2	1	1961	166-8	George Shepperson
Race	2	1	1960/61	72-3	L. H. Gann
RLJ	--	30	1961	56-8	R. Robinson

111   Clements, Frank
      RHODESIA; A STUDY OF THE DETERIORATION OF A WHITE SOCIETY.
      New York, Praeger, 1969.

      RHODESIA: THE COURSE TO COLLISION.
      London, Pall Mall Press, 1969.

Af Af	69	277	1970	406-8	Kenneth Kirkwood
Af HS	3	1	1970	481-6	L. H. Gann
Af StR	13	1	1970	127-33	L. H. Gann
JMAS	8	1	1970	164-7	Barry M. Schutz
Race	11	3	1969/70	381-2	James Barber

112   Cohen, William B.
      RULERS OF EMPIRE: THE FRENCH COLONIAL SERVICE IN AFRICA.
      Stanford, Hoover Institution Press, 1971.

Afr	42	4	1972	345-6	Hubert Deschamps
Af Af	71	284	1972	343-4	Robert Heussler
Af SR	--	15	1973	402-3	James R. Finucane
Af St	34	3	1975	212-4	Keith Gottschalk
AHR	80	3	1975	700-1	David E. Gardinier
Hist	58	193	1973	326	Peter Hatton
IJAHS	5	4	1972	676-80	Yves Person
JAH	14	3	1973	527	Rita Cruise O'Brien
JMAS	10	3	1972	484-6	Walter W. Bowring

113   Cole, Sonia Mary
THE PREHISTORY OF EAST AFRICA.
Harmondsworth, Middlesex, Penguin Books, 1954.

THE PREHISTORY OF EAST AFRICA. INTROD. BY RICHARD CARRINGTON.
New York, Macmillan, 1963.
London, Weidenfeld and Nicolson, 1964 (c1963).

Afr	26	1	1956	92-3	G. W. B. Huntingford
JAH	2	1	1961	153-4	Bridget Allchin
JAH	6	1	1965	123-5	Neville Chittick

114   Coleman, James Smoot
NIGERIA: BACKGROUND TO NATIONALISM.
Berkeley, University of California Press, 1958.

Afr	30	2	1960	189-91	Lucy Mair
AHR	64	3	1958/59	636-7	Vernon McKay
JAH	1	1	1960	180-1	John Flint
RLJ	--	25	1959	79-82	A. H. St. J. Wood

115   Collins, Robert O.
KING LEOPOLD, ENGLAND, AND THE UPPER NILE, 1899-1909.
New Haven, Yale University Press, 1968.

Af Af	68	271	1969	161-2	Iain Smith
Af HS	2	2	1969	345-7	Roger T. Anstey
AHR	75	4	1969/70	1083-4	Harold G. Marcus
BSOAS	32	3	1969	675-6	P. M. Holt
EHR	85	336	1970	627	Roger T. Anstey
HJ	13	3	1970	562-4	A. S. Kanya-Forstner
Hist	55	183	1970	154-5	E. Halladay
JAH	11	2	1970	287-8	J. R. Gray

116   Collins, Robert O.
LAND BEYOND THE RIVERS; THE SOUTHERN SUDAN, 1898-1918.
New Haven, Yale University Press, 1971.

Af Af	72	286	1973	87-8	Iain R. Smith
AHR	77	5	1972	1491-2	Irene L. Gendzier
BSOAS	35	3	1972	676-8	Gabriel Warburg
EHR	88	347	1973	465-6	P. E. H. Hair
Hist	57	189	1972	155-6	Peter Hatton
IJAHS	6	3	1973	533-4	Peter Mellini
JAH	14	1	1973	174-5	Michael Twaddle

Collins, Robert O.

117   Collins, Robert O.
       THE SOUTHERN SUDAN, 1883–1898, A STRUGGLE FOR CONTROL.
       New Haven, Yale University Press, 1962.

       AHR   68   2   1962/63 534–5   Ann Beck
       JAH   5   1   1964   149–50   Richard Gray

118   Cookey, Sylvanus John Sodienye
       BRITAIN AND THE CONGO QUESTION 1885–1913.
       London, Longmans, 1968.
       New York, Humanities Press, 1968.

       Af Af   69   277 1970   405–6   Suzanne Miers
       Af HS   2   2   1969   339–41   Douglas L. Wheeler
       BSOAS   32   2   1969   465   Anthony Atmore
       JAH   10   3   1969   509–11   Ruth Slade

119   Coquery-Vidrovitch, Catherine
       BRAZZA ET LA PRISE DE POSSESSION DU CONGO; LA MISSION DE
       L'OUEST AFRICAIN, 1883–1885. INTROD. ET CHOIX DE TEXTES PAR
       CATHERINE COQUERY-VIDROVITCH, AVEC LE CONCOURS DE OTTO GOLLN-
       HOFER, ET AL.
       Paris, Mouton, 1969.

       Afr   40   3   1970   286   Hubert Deschamps
       Af HS   4   1   1971   151–2   Roger Anstey

120   Corfield, F. D.
       HISTORICAL SURVEY OF THE ORIGINS AND GROWTH OF MAU MAU.
       London, H. M. Stationery Office, 1960.

       Afr   31   2   1961   186–7   John Middleton
       JAH   2   1   1961   168–70   F. B. Welbourn

121   Cornevin, Robert
       HISTOIRE DE L'AFRIQUE.
       Paris, Payot, 1962.

       Afr   33   3   1963   277   R. Mauny
       AHR   68   4   1962/63 1067–8   David E. Gardinier
       IJAHS   8   3   1975   468–70   Spencer H. Brown
       JAH   8   2   1967   349–51   Richard Gray
       JAH   16   3   1975   461–2   Terence Ranger

Crowder, Michael

122   Cornevin, Robert
       HISTOIRE DES PEUPLES DE L'AFRIQUE NOIRE.
       Paris, Berger-Levrault, 1960.

Afr	31	3	1961	291	Hubert Deschamps
JAH	1	2	1960	313-5	D. H. Jones

123   Cornevin, Robert
       HISTOIRE DU DAHOMEY. AVEC 10 CARTES, 1 CROQUIS ET 35 PHOTOS.
       Paris, Berger-Levrault, 1962.

Afr	33	4	1963	375	C. W. Newbury
AHR	71	1	1965/66	272-3	J. L. Hymans

124   Cornevin, Robert
       HISTOIRE DU TOGO. PRÉF. DE HUBERT DESCHAMPS. AVEC 16 CARTES
       ET 46 PHOTOS.
       Paris, Berger-Levrault, 1959.

Afr	30	2	1960	196	Hubert Deschamps
JAH	1	2	1960	317-9	J. D. Fage

125   Creighton, Thomas Richmond Mandell
       THE ANATOMY OF PARTNERSHIP; SOUTHERN RHODESIA AND THE CENTRAL
       AFRICAN FEDERATION.
       London, Faber and Faber, 1960.

       SOUTHERN RHODESIA AND THE CENTRAL AFRICAN FEDERATION; THE
       ANATOMY OF PARTNERSHIP.
       New York, Praeger, 1961 (c1960).

Af Af	60	238	1961	110-1	S. S.
Af St	20	2	1961	141-2	S. T.
JAH	2	1	1961	166-8	George Shepperson
Race	2	2	1960/61	84	Basil Davidson

126   Crowder, Michael
       REVOLT IN BUSSA; A STUDY OF BRITISH 'NATIVE ADMINISTRATION' IN
       NIGERIAN BORGU, 1902-1935.
       Evanston, Northwestern University Press, 1973.

AHR	80	1	1975	152-3	L. Gray Cowan
BSOAS	37	3	1974	733-5	Mervyn Hiskett
Hist	59	196	1974	307	Christopher Fyfe
JAH	15	3	1974	511-3	David Craig Dorward

Crowder, Michael

127   Crowder, Michael
       SENEGAL; A STUDY IN FRENCH ASSIMILATION POLICY.
       London, New York, Oxford University Press, 1962.

Afr	33	2	1963	167-8	H. Deschamps
Af Af	61	245	1962	352	-----
Af Af	67	268	1968	265-6	C. W. Newbury
AHR	68	2	1962/63	456-7	David E. Gardinier
EHR	85	334	1970	204	George Shepperson
JAH	4	2	1963	307	Douglas Johnson
JMAS	1	1	1963	113-5	David Apter
Race	9	3	1967/68	384-5	Claude Welch

128   Crowder, Michael
       THE STORY OF NIGERIA.
       London, Faber and Faber, 1962; rev. ed., 1966.

       A SHORT HISTORY OF NIGERIA.
       New York, Praeger, 1962; rev. ed., 1966.

Afr	33	2	1963	161-2	A. H. M. Kirk-Greene
Af Af	63	253	1964	312	-----
AHR	69	1	1963/64	140-1	Robert I. Rotberg
EHR	79	310	1964	198-9	J. D. Hargreaves
Hist	48	164	1963	412-4	J. D. Fage
JAH	4	1	1963	133-4	John Flint
JMAS	6	3	1968	450-1	Oluwadare Aguda
Race	4	1	1962/63	127	H. A. S. Johnston

129   Crowder, Michael
       WEST AFRICA UNDER COLONIAL RULE.
       Evanston, Northwestern University Press, 1968.
       London, Hutchinson, 1968.

Afr	39	1	1969	81	Hubert Deschamps
Af Af	68	272	1969	271-2	D. H. Jones
Af HS	2	2	1969	367-8	William B. Cohen
Af SR	--	7	1969	566-7	Fola Soremekun
AHR	74	5	1968/69	1679-80	Wolfe W. Schmokel
Hist	55	184	1970	316-7	Freda Harcourt
JAH	10	3	1969	493-5	Henri Brunschwig
JMAS	7	3	1969	542-3	Fred L. Hadsel
Race	10	3	1968/69	396-7	Billy J. Dudley

130 Crowder, Michael
WEST AFRICAN RESISTANCE: THE MILITARY RESPONSE TO COLONIAL
OCCUPATION. EDITED BY MICHAEL CROWDER.
London, Hutchinson, 1971.
New York, Africana Pub. Corp., 1971.

Afr	42	1	1972	65-6	Jack Goody
Af Af	71	283	1972	206-7	Boniface I. Obichere
BSOAS	35	2	1972	419-21	Mervyn Hiskett
Hist	58	193	1973	327	David Birmingham
IJAHS	5	1	1972	102-6	John Flint
JAH	13	1	1972	161-3	John Miles

131 Cruise O'Brien, Donal Brian
THE MOURIDES OF SENEGAL: THE POLITICAL AND ECONOMIC ORGANIZA-
TION OF AN ISLAMIC BROTHERHOOD.
Oxford, Clarendon Press, 1971.

Afr	43	4	1973	366-7	Jean Copans
Af Af	71	283	1972	204-6	R. A. Joseph
EHR	87	345	1972	908-9	P. E. H. Hair
Hist	57	189	1972	158-9	Humphrey J. Fisher
IJAHS	5	1	1972	148-9	Lucy C. Behrman
IJAHS	5	4	1972	637-58	Louis Brenner
JAH	13	1	1972	157-8	Martin A. Klein
JMAS	11	4	1973	675-81	Clement Cottingham

132 Cruise O'Brien, Rita
WHITE SOCIETY IN BLACK AFRICA: THE FRENCH OF SENEGAL.
London, Faber and Faber, Ltd., 1972.
Evanston, Northwestern University Press, 1972.

EHR	88	348	1973	686	R. W. Johnson
Hist	58	193	1973	328	A. S. Kanya-Forstner
IJAHS	7	1	1974	158-9	L. H. Gann
JAH	14	1	1973	164-5	Margaret Peil
JMAS	11	3	1973	492-6	P-Kiven Tunteng

133 Crummey, Donald
PRIESTS AND POLITICIANS: PROTESTANT AND CATHOLIC MISSIONS IN
ORTHODOX ETHIOPIA, 1830-1868.
Oxford, Clarendon Press, 1972.

Afr	44	4	1974	426-7	Hector Blackhurst
BSOAS	37	3	1974	681-2	A. K. Irvine

Curtin, Philip D.

(Crummey, Donald)

IJAHS	8	2	1975	338-40	Edward Simone
JAH	15	1	1974	156-8	Tadesse Tamrat
JMAS	13	2	1975	361-6	William A. Shack

134 Curtin, Philip D.
THE ATLANTIC SLAVE TRADE; A CENSUS.
Madison, University of Wisconsin Press, 1969.

Afr	40	4	1970	395-9	Hubert Deschamps
Af Af	70	279	1971	176-7	W. E. Minchinton
Af HS	3	2	1970	453-5	James A. Rawley
Af St	31	2	1972	139-40	M. D. W. Jeffreys
Af StR	13	1	1970	143-4	Thomas P. Govan
AHR	75	7	1969/70	2011	Eugene D. Genovese
JAH	11	3	1970	457-9	Roger Anstey
Race	13	1	1971/72	119-21	Donald Wood

135 Curtin, Philip D.
THE IMAGE OF AFRICA; BRITISH IDEAS AND ACTION, 1780-1850.
Madison, University of Wisconsin Press, 1964.

Afr	34	3	1964	282-4	C. W. Newbury
Af Af	63	252	1964	242-3	Hilary Blood
Af Af	65	258	1966	97-8	I. Bindiga
AHR	70	1	1964/65	165-7	Robert I. Rotberg
Hist	50	170	1965	398-9	John D. Hargreaves
JAH	5	3	1964	461-2	Philip Mason
JMAS	2	4	1964	591-4	Asa Briggs
Race	7	1	1965/66	87-9	Michael Banton

136 Daaku, Kwame Yeboa
TRADE AND POLITICS ON THE GOLD COAST, 1600-1720: A STUDY OF
THE AFRICAN REACTION TO EUROPEAN TRADE.
London, Clarendon Press, 1970.

Afr	42	1	1972	73	Margaret Priestley
Af HS	4	3	1971	720-4	H. M. Feinberg
AHR	76	3	1971	813-4	Daniel F. McCall
BSOAS	35	1	1972	187-8	D. H. Jones
EHR	87	342	1972	187-8	Christopher Fyfe
EHR	87	343	1972	409-10	D. K. Fieldhouse
Hist	56	187	1971	310	A. J. H. Latham
JAH	12	2	1971	330-1	Graham W. Irwin

137   Dalby, David
      LANGUAGE AND HISTORY IN AFRICA: A VOLUME OF COLLECTED PAPERS
      PRESENTED TO THE LONDON SEMINAR ON LANGUAGE AND HISTORY IN
      AFRICA (HELD AT THE SCHOOL OF ORIENTAL AND AFRICAN STUDIES,
      1967-69), EDITED BY DAVID DALBY.
      London, Cass, 1970.

Afr	43	1	1973	81-2	Pierre Alexandre
Af St	31	1	1972	46-9	William E. Welmers
BSOAS	35	3	1972	670-2	Robert Hetzron
IJAHS	5	2	1972	316-8	Edgar A. Gregersen
JAH	12	3	1971	493-6	Jan Vansina

138   Davenport, T. R. H.
      THE AFRIKANER BOND; THE HISTORY OF A SOUTH AFRICAN POLITICAL
      PARTY, 1880-1911.
      Cape Town, New York, Oxford University Press, 1966.

Af Af	66	264	1967	279-80	D. M. van der Schreuder
AHR	73	2	1967/68	562-3	Jeffrey Butler
BSOAS	30	3	1967	739-40	Anthony Atmore
JAH	12	2	1971	334-5	May Katzen

139   Davidson, Basil
      AFRICA: HISTORY OF A CONTINENT; WITH PHOTOGRAPHS BY WERNER
      FORMAN.
      London, Weidenfeld and Nicolson, 1966.
      New York, Macmillan, 1966.

Afr	37	3	1967	365-6	R. M.
Af Af	66	264	1967	257-8	Brian Macdona
Race	8	4	1966/67	422-3	Robert I. Rotberg

140   Davidson, Basil
      THE AFRICAN GENIUS; AN INTRODUCTION TO AFRICAN CULTURAL AND
      SOCIAL HISTORY.
      Boston, Little, Brown, 1970 (c1969).

      THE AFRICANS: AN ENTRY TO CULTURAL HISTORY.
      Harlow, Longmans, 1969.

Af HS	4	1	1971	200-1	David Birmingham
JMAS	10	3	1972	477-9	Boris S. Erassov

Davidson, Basil

141   Davidson, Basil
      BLACK MOTHER; AFRICA: THE YEARS OF TRIAL.
      London, V. Gollancz, 1961.

      BLACK MOTHER; THE YEARS OF THE AFRICAN SLAVE TRADE.
      Boston, Little, Brown, 1961.

      JAH   3   3   1962   509-11   C. R. Boxer
      Race   3   2   1961/62   92-3   Richard Gray

142   Davidson, Basil
      OLD AFRICA REDISCOVERED.
      London, Gollancz, 1959.

      THE LOST CITIES OF AFRICA.
      Boston, Little, Brown, 1959.

      Afr   30   3   1960   295-6   R. Mauny
      JAH   1   1   1960   149-51   Raymond Mauny
      Race   1   2   1959/60   77-80   Philip Mason

143   Delavignette, Robert Louis
      ... LES VRAIS CHEFS DE L'EMPIRE.   (censored edition)
      Paris, Gallimard, 1939.

      SERVICE AFRICAIN.   (complete edition)
      Paris, Gallimard, 1946.

      FREEDOM AND AUTHORITY IN FRENCH WEST AFRICA.
      London, New York, published for the International African In-
      stitute by the Oxford University Press, 1950.

      Afr   21   3   1951   246-7   L. P. Mair
      Af Af   50   199 1951   170-1   H. V. L. S.
      Af St   10   2   1951   57-8   L. L.

144   Denoon, Donald
      A GRAND ILLUSION; THE FAILURE OF IMPERIAL POLICY IN THE TRANS-
      VAAL COLONY DURING THE PERIOD OF RECONSTRUCTION 1900-1905.
      London, Longman, 1973.

      Af Af   73   293 1974   476-7   R. Hyam

Deschamps, Hubert Jules

145   Denoon, Donald
      SOUTHERN AFRICA SINCE 1800, BY DONALD DENOON, WITH BALAM NYEKO
      AND THE ADVICE OF J. B. WEBSTER.
      London, Longman, 1972.
      New York, Praeger, 1973 (c1972).

      Af SR   -- 16   1973   509-11   Timothy M. Shaw
      JAH   15 3   1974   491-3   Shula Marks

146   Deschamps, Hubert Jules
      L'AFRIQUE NOIRE PRÉCOLONIALE.
      Paris, Presses Universitaires de France, 1962.

      Afr   34 1   1964   64   George Shepperson

147   Deschamps, Hubert Jules
      HISTOIRE DE LA TRAITE DES NOIRS DE L'ANTIQUITÉ À NOS JOURS.
      Paris, Fayard, 1972.

      Afr   43 2   1973   158-9   J. D. Fage
      JAH   14 1   1973   156-7   Roger Anstey

148   Deschamps, Hubert Jules
      HISTOIRE DE MADAGASCAR.
      Paris, Berger-Levrault, 1960.

      Afr   31 3   1961   283-5   Robert F. Gray
      Afr   45 2   1975   209-10   M. Bloch
      JAH   1   2   1960   319-21   Roland Oliver

149   Deschamps, Hubert Jules
      LES MÉTHODES ET LES DOCTRINES COLONIALES DE LA FRANCE, DU XVIe
      SIÈCLE À NOS JOURS.
      Paris, A. Colin, 1953.

      Hist   40 138-9 1955   158   A. Cobban

150   Deschamps, Hubert Jules
      LE SÉNÉGAL ET LA GAMBIE.
      Paris, Presses Universitaires de France, 1964.

      Afr   37 3   1967   363-5   Michael Crowder
      JAH   5   3   1964   469   John D. Hargreaves

Diké, Kenneth Onwuka

151   Diké, Kenneth Onwuka
      TRADE AND POLITICS IN THE NIGER DELTA, 1830–1855; AN INTRODUC-
      TION TO THE ECONOMIC AND POLITICAL HISTORY OF NIGERIA.
      Oxford, Clarendon Press, 1956.

Afr	27	1	1957	83–5	G. I. Jones
Af Af	55	219	1956	150–1	J. Ade Ajayi
Af St	16	3	1957	187–90	M. D. W. Jeffreys
AHR	62	1	1956/57	197–8	Vernon McKay
EHR	72	282	1957	191–2	Freda Wolfson
Hist	43	147	1958	66–7	Eveline Martin

152   Dotson, Floyd and Lillian O.
      THE INDIAN MINORITY OF ZAMBIA, RHODESIA, AND MALAWI.
      New Haven, London, Yale University Press, 1968.

Af Af	71	282	1972	98–100	James S. Read
Af SR	--	7	1969	555–8	Ronald Frankenberg
Af St	29	2	1970	152–4	Jessica Kuper
BSOAS	32	2	1969	448–9	A. C. Mayer
CSSH	12	2	1970	233–6	H. S. Morris
JAH	9	4	1968	666–7	Bridglal Pachai
JMAS	7	4	1969	762–3	Sukhi Singh
Race	10	4	1968/69	534–5	J. S. Mangat

153   Dudley, Billy J.
      PARTIES AND POLITICS IN NORTHERN NIGERIA.
      London, Cass, 1968.

Afr	39	2	1969	197–8	A. H. M. Kirk-Greene
Af Af	68	271	1969	167–8	Murray Last
Af HS	3	1	1970	191–2	J. A. Ballard
Af St	29	2	1970	144–6	Noam J. Pines
JAH	10	2	1969	340–1	Richard Rathbone
JMAS	7	4	1969	756–8	John A. Ballard
Race	10	3	1968/69	394–5	C. E. Welch

154   Duffy, James
      PORTUGAL IN AFRICA.
      Cambridge, Harvard University Press, 1962.
      Harmondsworth, Middlesex, Penguin Books, 1962.

Af Af	61	245	1962	351	-----
AHR	68	3	1962/63	810–1	Bailey W. Diffie
Race	4	1	1962/63	127–8	Clifford J. Parsons

Esterhuyse, J. H.

155   Duffy, James
      PORTUGUESE AFRICA.
      Cambridge, Harvard University Press, 1959.

Afr	30	3	1960	284-5	Guy Atkins
Af Af	59	234	1960	76-7	D. H. S.
Af St	19	3	1960	137	Julius Lewin
AHR	65	2	1959/60	377-8	Vernon McKay
BSOAS	23	1	1960	189-90	Roland Oliver
EHR	75	297	1960	741-2	J. D. Hargreaves
Hist	45	155	1960	281-3	Roland Oliver
JAH	1	1	1960	153-4	Eric Axelson

156   Duly, Leslie Clement
      BRITISH LAND POLICY AT THE CAPE, 1795-1844: A STUDY OF ADMIN-
      ISTRATIVE PROCEDURES IN THE EMPIRE.
      Durham, N. C., Duke University Press, 1968.

Af Af	68	273	1969	371-2	T. R. H. Davenport
Af HS	2	1	1969	141-3	Maynard W. Swanson
AHR	74	3	1968/69	987-8	Jeffrey Butler
Hist	54	182	1969	464	D. A. Farnie
JAH	11	1	1970	152-3	M. Katzen

157   THE EARLY HISTORY OF MALAWI; EDITED BY BRIDGLAL PACHAI.
      London, Longman, 1972.

Af Af	72	286	1973	95-6	P. Redmond
BSOAS	36	2	1973	510-1	Richard Gray
IJAHS	7	1	1974	166-8	Roderick J. Macdonald
JAH	13	3	1972	511-3	Terence Ranger

158   Ekechi, F. K.
      MISSIONARY ENTERPRISE AND RIVALRY IN IGBOLAND, 1857-1914.
      London, Cass, 1972.

Af Af	72	287	1973	207-8	Elizabeth Isichei
JAH	14	1	1973	154-5	C. M. Cooke

159   Esterhuyse, J. H.
      SOUTH WEST AFRICA, 1880-1894: THE ESTABLISHMENT OF GERMAN
      AUTHORITY IN SOUTH WEST AFRICA.
      Cape Town, C. Struik, 1968.

Evans-Pritchard, Edward Evan

(Esterhuyse, J. H.)

JAH	10	1	1969	185-6	Helmut Bley
JMAS	6	4	1968	600-3	Franz Ansprenger

160   Evans-Pritchard, Edward Evan
THE AZANDE: HISTORY AND POLITICAL INSTITUTIONS.
Oxford, Clarendon Press, 1971.

AHR	80	4	1975	1021-2	Jan Vansina
BSOAS	36	3	1973	732-3	Abner Cohen
JAH	13	2	1972	329-32	Pierre Kalck

161   Fagan, Brian M.
SOUTHERN AFRICA DURING THE IRON AGE.
London, Thames and Hudson, 1965.
New York, F. A. Praeger, 1965.

Afr	36	4	1966	466	Roger Summers
Af Af	66	264	1967	256-7	Frank Willett
JAH	7	3	1966	510-1	Roland Oliver

162   Fage, J. D.
AN ATLAS OF AFRICAN HISTORY.
London, E. Arnold, 1958.
(Reprinted with amendments, 1963.)

Afr	29	1	1959	98-100	P. C. Lloyd
Af St	18	2	1959	102-3	E. A.
BSOAS	22	1	1959	180-1	G. W. B. Huntingford
EHR	74	291	1959	383-4	George Shepperson
Hist	44	150	1959	92-3	George Bennett
JAH	1	1	1960	172	Henri Brunschwig
Race	1	1	1959/60	85-6	Donald Wood
RLJ	--	24	1958	90-2	R. J. Apthorpe

163   Fage, J. D.
GHANA: A HISTORICAL INTERPRETATION.
Madison, University of Wisconsin Press, 1959.

Af Af	59	237	1960	343-4	Joseph Amamos
Af St	20	1	1961	85-6	A. K. Fryer
AHR	66	1	1960/61	186-7	Melvin D. Kennedy
EHR	76	299	1961	375-6	J. D. Hargreaves
JAH	1	2	1960	323-5	Ivor Wilks

164   Fage, J. D.
       AN INTRODUCTION TO THE HISTORY OF WEST AFRICA.
       Cambridge, University Press, 1955.

       A HISTORY OF WEST AFRICA: AN INTRODUCTORY SURVEY.   4TH ED.
       London, Cambridge U.P., 1969.

Afr	26	4	1956	413	Cherry Gertzel
Afr	40	2	1970	175	Robert Smith
Af Af	55	219	1956	147-8	W. A. G. M.
Af Af	59	237	1960	344	T. O. Elias
Af HS	3	1	1970	225-9	Daniel F. McCall
Af St	31	1	1972	41-3	C. C. Saunders
Af StR	13	1	1970	138-9	Raymond C. Ganga
BSOAS	18	2	1956	398	D. Jones

165   Fallers, Lloyd A.
       BANTU BUREAUCRACY; A STUDY OF INTEGRATION AND CONFLICT IN THE
       POLITICAL INSTITUTIONS OF AN EAST AFRICAN PEOPLE.
       Cambridge, published for the East African Institute of Social
       Research by W. Heffer, 195-.

       BANTU BUREAUCRACY; A CENTURY OF POLITICAL EVOLUTION AMONG THE
       BASOGA OF UGANDA.
       Chicago, University of Chicago Press, 1965.

Afr	27	2	1957	197-8	L. P. Mair
Af St	17	1	1958	55-6	Eileen Jenson Krige
JMAS	4	3	1966	349-57	Robert L. Tignor
RLJ	--	23	1958	62-5	E. Colson

166   Fallers, Lloyd A., ed.
       THE KING'S MEN; LEADERSHIP AND STATUS IN BUGANDA ON THE EVE OF
       INDEPENDENCE. WITH A FOREWORD BY A. I. RICHARDS.
       London, New York, published on behalf of the East African In-
       stitute of Social Research, by Oxford University Press, 1964.

Afr	34	4	1964	377-9	Peter C. W. Gutkind
Af Af	64	254	1965	56-7	Edwin Ardener
BSOAS	28	2	1965	438-9	I. M. Lewis
JAH	6	2	1965	237-9	D. A. Low
JMAS	4	1	1966	120-4	Matia Kiwanuka
JMAS	4	3	1966	349-57	Robert L. Tignor
Race	5	4	1963/64	105-6	George Bennett

Fallers, Lloyd A.

167   Fallers, Lloyd A.
LAW WITHOUT PRECEDENT; LEGAL IDEAS IN ACTION IN THE COURTS OF
COLONIAL BUSOGA.
Chicago, University of Chicago Press, 1969.

| Afr | 41 | 4 | 1971 | 328-9 | Ian Hamnett |
| BSOAS | 34 | 1 | 1971 | 199-201 | A. N. Allott |

168   Fanon, Frantz
LES DAMNÉS DE LA TERRE. PRÉF. DE JEAN PAUL SARTRE.
Paris, F. Maspero, 1961.

THE WRETCHED OF THE EARTH; PREFACE BY JEAN-PAUL SARTRE.
TRANSLATED FROM THE FRENCH BY CONSTANCE FARRINGTON.
London, Macgibbon and McKee, 1963.

| JMAS | 1 | 3 | 1963 | 403-5 | Franz Ansprenger |
| JMAS | 6 | 4 | 1968 | 543-56 | G. K. Grohs |

169   Fanon, Frantz
PEAU NOIRE, MASQUES BLANCS. PRÉF. DE FRANCIS JEANSON.
Paris, Éditions du Seuil, 1952.

PEAU NOIRE, MASQUES BLANCS. PRÉF. (1952) ET POSTFACE (1965)
DE FRANCIS JEANSON.
Paris, Éditions de Seuil, 1965 (c1952).

BLACK SKIN, WHITE MASKS. TRANSLATED BY CHARLES LAM MARKMANN.
New York, Grove Press, 1967.

| JMAS | 6 | 4 | 1968 | 543-56 | G. K. Grohs |

170   Feit, Edward
AFRICAN OPPOSITION IN SOUTH AFRICA; THE FAILURE OF PASSIVE
RESISTANCE.
Stanford, Hoover Institution on War, Revolution, and Peace,
Stanford University, 1967.

Afr	39	1	1969	94-5	Pierre L. van den Berghe
Af Af	68	271	1969	174-6	D. M. Van der H. Schreuder
Af HS	2	1	1969	154-6	K. A. Heard

171   Feit, Edward
SOUTH AFRICA: THE DYNAMICS OF THE AFRICAN NATIONAL CONGRESS.
London, New York, Oxford University Press, 1962.

Fitch, Robert Beck

(Feit, Edward)
JAH	4	1	1963	146-7	T. R. H. Davenport
JMAS	1	4	1963	548-9	S. Trapido
Race	4	2	1962/63	81	Mary Benson

172   Ferkiss, Victor C.
AFRICA'S SEARCH FOR IDENTITY.
New York, Braziller, 1966.

| Af Af | 69 | 277 | 1970 | 398-9 | Wieland Jaeger |
| JMAS | 5 | 1 | 1967 | 144-7 | Mazi Ray Ofoegbu |

173   Fisher, Allan George Bernard
SLAVERY AND MUSLIM SOCIETY IN AFRICA: THE INSTITUTION IN
SAHARAN AND SUDANIC AFRICA, AND THE TRANS-SAHARAN TRADE, BY
ALLAN G. B. FISHER AND HUMPHREY J. FISHER.
London, C. Hurst, 1970.
Garden City, N. Y., Doubleday, 1971 (c1970).

Afr	41	3	1971	260	Hubert Deschamps
Af Af	71	284	1972	339-40	Michael Brett
Af StR	16	3	1973	457-8	Raymond Ganga
BSOAS	35	3	1972	672-3	Ivan Hrbek
Hist	59	196	1974	309-10	J. D. Fage
JAH	14	3	1973	509-10	Anthony Atmore

174   Fisher, Humphrey J.
AHMADIYYAH; A STUDY IN CONTEMPORARY ISLĀM ON THE WEST AFRICAN
COAST.
London, published for the Nigerian Institute of Social and
Economic Research by Oxford University Press, 1963.

Afr	33	4	1963	373-4	Jean-Claude Froelich
Af Af	63	251	1964	150-1	E. G. Parrinder
BSOAS	27	2	1964	492-3	J. Schacht

175   Fitch, Robert Beck
GHANA; END OF AN ILLUSION, BY BOB FITCH AND MARY OPPENHEIMER.
New York, Monthly Review Press, 1966.

| JMAS | 4 | 3 | 1966 | 381-4 | Thomas Hodgkin |
| JMAS | 7 | 1 | 1969 | 107-30 | Jon Kraus |

Flint, John E.

176   Flint, John E.
       NIGERIA AND GHANA.
       Englewood Cliffs, N. J., Prentice-Hall, 1966.

       AHR   72   3   1966/67   1046-7   Hans E. Panofsky
       JAH   8   3   1967   541-6   Adu Boahen

177   Flint, John E.
       SIR GEORGE GOLDIE AND THE MAKING OF NIGERIA.
       London, Oxford University Press, 1960.

       Afr   31   4   1961   394-5   A. H. M. Kirk-Greene
       Af Af 60 241   1961   546-7   Iain Gunn
       AHR   66   3   1960/61   703-5   Garland G. Parker
       BSOAS 24   2   1961   403-4   D. H. Jones
       Hist   46 157   1961   180-2   J. D. Fage
       JAH   2   2   1961   332-7   Kenneth Robinson

178   Foltz, William J.
       FROM FRENCH WEST AFRICA TO THE MALI FEDERATION.
       New Haven, Yale University Press, 1965.

       Af Af 65 261   1966   357-8   Teresa Hayter
       JAH   7   1   1966   163-4   C. M. Le Quesne
       JMAS   3   3   1965   443-4   Paul Semonin

179   Forde, Cyril Daryll
       WEST AFRICAN KINGDOMS IN THE NINETEENTH CENTURY; EDITED WITH
       AN INTRODUCTION BY DARYLL FORDE AND P. M. KABERRY.
       London, Oxford U.P., for the International African Institute,
       1967.

       Afr   39   1   1969   79-80   J. D. Fage
       Af Af 67 269   1968   365-7   Edwin Ardener
       AHR   73   3   1967/68   872-3   Graham Irwin
       BSOAS 31   3   1968   657-8   D. H. Jones
       Hist   54 180   1969   152-3   A. G. Hopkins
       IJAHS   5   4   1972   692-3   Martin A. Klein
       JAH   9   2   1968   319-29   P. C. Lloyd
       JMAS   8   1   1970   117-21   Kenneth C. Wylie

180   FRANCE AND BRITAIN IN AFRICA: IMPERIAL RIVALRY AND COLONIAL
       RULE. EDITED BY PROSSER GIFFORD AND WILLIAM ROGER LOUIS.
       New Haven, Yale University Press, 1971.

Fynn, John Kofi

(FRANCE AND BRITAIN IN AFRICA:)
Af Af	72	289	1973	447-8	Iain R. Smith
AHR	80	1	1975	150-2	Graham W. Irwin
EHR	88	349	1973	864-6	Roger Bullen
Hist	58	193	1973	324	Peter Hatton
IJAHS	7	1	1974	162-4	Eunice A. Charles
JAH	15	1	1974	141-5	Michael Crowder
JMAS	13	1	1975	168-71	L. Adele Jinadu

181 Freeman-Grenville, Greville Stewart Parker
THE MEDIEVAL HISTORY OF THE COAST OF TANGANYIKA, WITH SPECIAL
REFERENCE TO RECENT ARCHEOLOGICAL DISCOVERIES.
London, New York, Oxford University Press, 1962.

Afr	33	2	1963	158-60	W. H. Whiteley
AHR	69	1	1963/64	223-4	Norman R. Bennett
BSOAS	27	2	1964	491-2	Kenneth Ingham
EHR	79	313	1964	834	George Shepperson
Hist	48	164	1964	410	Roland Oliver
JAH	4	2	1963	294-6	Roland Oliver
Race	6	2	1964/65	159-62	Richard Gray
RLJ	--	33	1963	99-100	M. Newitt

182 Furse, Sir Ralph Dolignon
AUCUPARIUS; RECOLLECTIONS OF A RECRUITING OFFICER. WITH A
FOREWORD BY THE MARQUESS OF SALISBURY.
London, New York, Oxford University Press, 1962.

Af Af	61	245	1962	327	Hilary Blood
JMAS	1	4	1963	558-60	Alec Dickson

183 Fyfe, Christopher
A HISTORY OF SIERRA LEONE.
London, Oxford University Press, 1962.

Af Af	62	246	1963	76	Hilary Blood
AHR	68	3	1962/63	752	Vernon McKay
BSOAS	26	1	1963	225	D. H. Jones
EHR	79	312	1964	570-1	J. D. Hargreaves
Hist	50	168	1965	131-2	J. D. Fage
JAH	6	3	1965	426-7	John E. Peterson

184 Fynn, John Kofi
ASANTE AND ITS NEIGHBOURS, 1700-1807.
Harlow, Longman, Evanston, Northwestern University Press, 1971.

Gailey, Harry A.

(Fynn, John Kofi)					
Af Af	72	288	1973	339-40	Kwame Arhin
IJAHS	7	1	1974	150-2	Margaret Priestley
JAH	13	3	1972	516-8	R. C. C. Law

185   Gailey, Harry A.
       A HISTORY OF THE GAMBIA.
       New York, Praeger, 1965.

Afr	35	3	1965	330	Christopher Fyfe
AHR	70	4	1964/65	1216	Arthur N. Cook
Hist	50	170	1965	395	K. G. Davies
JAH	6	3	1965	428-9	Florence Mahoney

186   Gailey, Harry A.
       THE ROAD TO ABA; A STUDY OF BRITISH ADMINISTRATIVE POLICY IN
       EASTERN NIGERIA.
       New York, New York University Press, 1970.

Afr	42	4	1972	355-6	G. I. Jones
Af StR	15	1	1972	139-45	David Northrup
AHR	77	3	1972	818-9	Henry S. Wilson
Hist	58	193	1973	327-8	Christopher Fyfe
JAH	16	1	1975	157-8	D. H. Jones
JMAS	10	2	1972	328-30	A. E. Afigbo

187   Gaitskell, Arthur
       GEZIRA; A STORY OF DEVELOPMENT IN THE SUDAN.
       London, Faber and Faber, 1959.

Afr	30	3	1960	287-8	K. M. Barbour
Af Af	59	236	1960	260-1	W. V. Blewett

188   Galbraith, John S.
       MACKINNON AND EAST AFRICA 1878-1895; A STUDY IN THE 'NEW IM-
       PERIALISM.'
       Cambridge, University Press, 1972.

Afr	44	1	1974	108-9	Michael Twaddle
Af StR	16	3	1973	452-4	James J. Cooke
AHR	78	4	1973	1112	Margaret Hay
BSOAS	36	2	1973	512-3	I. K. Orchardson
EHR	90	356	1975	675-6	P. E. H. Hair
Hist	59	195	1974	126	B. Porter
IJAHS	7	1	1974	175-8	R. C. Bridges

189   Galbraith, John S.
      RELUCTANT EMPIRE; BRITISH POLICY ON THE SOUTH AFRICAN FRONTIER,
      1834-1854.
      Berkeley, University of California Press, 1963.

Af Af	63	253	1964	312-3	-----
AHR	69	1	1963/64	141-2	Colin Rhys Lovell
EHR	80	316	1965	622-3	Philip S. Haffenden
HJ	8	1	1965	145-7	Eric A. Walker
Race	6	1	1964/65	78-9	W. M. Macmillan

190   Gale, Hubert P.
      UGANDA AND THE MILL HILL FATHERS.
      London, Macmillan, 1959.

Afr	30	2	1960	199	John Middleton
JAH	1	1	1960	163-6	Roland Oliver

191   Gann, Lewis H.
      THE BIRTH OF A PLURAL SOCIETY; THE DEVELOPMENT OF NORTHERN
      RHODESIA UNDER THE BRITISH SOUTH AFRICA COMPANY, 1894-1914.
      Manchester, published on behalf of the Rhodes-Livingstone In-
      stitute, Northern Rhodesia, by Manchester University Press,
      1958.

Af St	18	3	1959	151-2	Eric Stokes
Hist	44	150	1959	93-5	George Bennett
JAH	1	1	1960	159-63	J. D. Fage

192   Gann, Lewis H.
      BURDEN OF EMPIRE; AN APPRAISAL OF WESTERN COLONIALISM IN
      AFRICA SOUTH OF THE SAHARA, BY L. H. GANN AND PETER DUIGNAN.
      London, published for the Hoover Institution on War, Revolu-
      tion, and Peace by Pall Mall Press, 1968.
      New York, F. A. Praeger, 1967.

Af Af	68	272	1969	269-70	A. S. Kanya-Forstner
Af HS	2	2	1969	335-8	George Shepperson
AHR	74	2	1968/69	682-3	Robert O. Collins
Hist	55	184	1970	316-7	Freda Harcourt
JAH	10	2	1969	333-6	A. E. Atmore
JMAS	7	1	1969	168-70	George W. Baer
Race	10	2	1968/69	240-2	Christopher Fyfe

Gann, Lewis H.

193   Gann, Lewis H.
       COLONIALISM IN AFRICA, 1870-1960: EDITED BY L. H. GANN AND
       PETER DUIGNAN.
       VOL. 1. THE HISTORY AND POLITICS OF COLONIALISM, 1870-1914.
                ED. BY L. H. GANN AND PETER DUIGNAN.
       VOL. 2. THE HISTORY AND POLITICS OF COLONIALISM, 1914-1960.
                ED. BY L. H. GANN AND PETER DUIGNAN.
       VOL. 3. PROFILES OF CHANGE: AFRICAN SOCIETY AND COLONIAL
                RULE. ED. BY VICTOR TURNER.
       VOL. 4. THE ECONOMICS OF COLONIALISM. ED. BY PETER DUIGNAN
                AND L. H. GANN.
       VOL. 5. A BIBLIOGRAPHICAL GUIDE TO COLONIALISM IN SUB-SAHARAN
                AFRICA. BY PETER DUIGNAN AND L. H. GANN.
       London, Cambridge U.P., 1969-75.

NOTE:	Volume	reviewed	listed	before	journal	abbreviation
1	Afr	40	2	1970	179	Lucy Mair
1	Af HS	3	2	1970	496-9	Jeffrey Butler
2	Af HS	4	3	1971	711-4	Norman R. Bennett
1,2,3	Af SR	--	15	1973	393-5	Ian Henderson
5	Af SR	--	20	1975	826-8	Robin and Judy Palmer
1	Af St	31	1	1972	44-6	Noam J. Pines
1	Af StR	13	1	1970	134-7	Kenneth C. Wylie
2	Af StR	14	1	1971	129-36	Kenneth C. Wylie
5	Af StR	17	1	1974	276	Kenneth C. Wylie
1	AHR	75	5	1969/70	1498-9	Donald L. Wiedner
2,3	AHR	77	4	1972	1164-6	Marcia Wright
3	BSOAS	34	3	1971	662-3	P. H. Gulliver
1	EHR	86	338	1971	146-7	David Fieldhouse
2,3	EHR	87	343	1972	387-8	D. K. Fieldhouse
1	Hist	56	187	1971	312	A. S. Kanya-Forstner
2,3	Hist	57	191	1972	475-6	Freda Harcourt
5	Hist	60	199	1975	250	A. J. Hanna
3	IJAHS	5	2	1972	345-8	Martin Legassick
1	JAH	12	1	1971	159-62	D. A. Low
5	JAH	15	4	1974	699-700	Richard Gray
1	JMAS	8	2	1970	316-8	Alberta Macke
2	JMAS	9	4	1971	644-7	Semakula Kiwanuka
3	JMAS	10	2	1972	311-4	Dan R. Aronson
1	Race	11	4	1969/70	520-2	Robert I. Rotberg
2	Race	13	1	1971/72	114-6	Robert I. Rotberg
3	Race	13	2	1971/72	256-7	Robert I. Rotberg

194   Gann, Lewis H.
       A HISTORY OF NORTHERN RHODESIA, EARLY DAYS TO 1953.
       London, Chatto and Windus, 1964 (c1963).

Gérard-Libois, Jules

(Gann, Lewis H.)

AHR	70	3	1964/65	881	Arthur N. Cook
EHR	81	318	1966	210-1	George Shepperson
JAH	5	3	1964	455-6	T. O. Ranger
JMAS	5	3	1967	432-3	Otakar Hulec

195 Gann, Lewis H.
A HISTORY OF SOUTHERN RHODESIA; EARLY DAYS TO 1934.
London, Chatto and Windus, 1965.

Af Af	65	259	1966	178-80	Gilbert Rennie
AHR	72	2	1966/67	662-3	Donald L. Wiedner
EHR	82	325	1967	812-4	A. J. Hanna
JAH	7	3	1966	525-7	Richard Brown

196 Gann, Lewis H.
HUGGINS OF RHODESIA; THE MAN AND HIS COUNTRY, BY L. H. GANN
AND M. GELFAND.
London, Allen and Unwin, 1964.

AHR	71	2	1965/66	637-8	F. Parker
EHR	81	319	1966	441	Eric Stokes
Hist	51	171	1966	131-2	George Shepperson
JMAS	3	1	1965	140-3	John Hatch
Race	6	2	1964/65	152-8	Philip Mason

197 Garlick, Peter C.
AFRICAN TRADERS IN KUMASI.
African Business Series No. 1. Economic Research Division,
University College of Ghana, 1959.

Afr	30	2	1960	191	Arthur Hazlewood

198 Gérard-Libois, Jules
SÉCESSION AU KATANGA.
Bruxelles, Centre de recherche et d'information socio-
politiques, 1963.

KATANGA SECESSION. TRANSLATED BY REBECCA YOUNG.
Madison, University of Wisconsin Press, 1966.

Af Af	66	264	1967	272-4	T. R. Kanza
Af Af	68	273	1969	367-70	George Ivan Smith
Af St	26	4	1967	252-4	Carl van Hoogenbemt

Gertzel, Cherry J.

(Gérard-Libois, Jules)
AHR	73	1	1967/68	193–4	Lewis H. Gann
JAH	9	1	1968	180–2	Roger Anstey
JMAS	2	2	1964	323–4	Thomas R. Kanza
JMAS	5	4	1967	579–81	Franz Ansprenger
Race	11	1	1969/70	94–5	C. E. Welch

199 Gertzel, Cherry J.
THE POLITICS OF INDEPENDENT KENYA, 1963–8.
Evanston, Northwestern University Press, 1970.
London, Heinemann, 1970.
Nairobi, East African Pub. House, 1970.

JAH	12	3	1971	504–6	Kenneth King
JMAS	10	3	1972	481–4	Susanne D. Mueller

200 Gibson, Richard
AFRICAN LIBERATION MOVEMENTS: CONTEMPORARY STRUGGLES AGAINST
WHITE MINORITY RULE.
London, New York, Oxford University Press for the Institute of
Race Relations, 1972.

Af Af	71	285	1972	451–2	Timothy M. Shaw
Af StR	16	3	1973	469–70	Richard Dale
AHR	80	2	1975	454–5	Gwendolen M. Carter
IJAHS	5	4	1972	712–3	Edward Feit
JAH	15	1	1974	166–7	Martin Legassick
JMAS	11	1	1973	168–70	Thomas H. Henriksen
Race	15	1	1973/74	143–4	Robert I. Rotberg

201 Goldthorpe, J. E.
AN AFRICAN ÉLITE: MAKERERE COLLEGE STUDENTS 1922–1960.
Nairobi, London, published on behalf of the East African Insti-
tute of Social Research by Oxford U.P., 1965 (i.e., 1966).

Af Af	66	262	1967	64–6	Edwin Ardener
JMAS	3	4	1965	637–9	R. C. Pratt

202 Goodfellow, Clement Francis
GREAT BRITAIN AND SOUTH AFRICAN CONFEDERATION, 1870–1881.
Cape Town, New York, Oxford University Press, 1966.

Af Af	67	266	1968	81–2	D. M. van der H. Schreuder
Af St	28	1	1969	63–5	N. G. Garson

(Goodfellow, Clement Francis)

EHR	83	329	1968	868-9	A. F. McC. Madden
Hist	53	178	1968	298-9	Freda Harcourt
JAH	10	1	1969	183-5	Shula Marks

203 Goody, John Rankine
TECHNOLOGY, TRADITION, AND THE STATE IN AFRICA.
London, Oxford University Press, 1971.

Afr	41	4	1971	331-3	C. Meillassoux
Af StR	15	3	1972	529-30	Edward I. Steinhart
BSOAS	35	2	1972	444	A. N. Allott
IJAHS	7	3	1974	537-40	Daniel F. McCall
JAH	12	3	1971	492-3	Roland Oliver
JMAS	10	2	1972	309-10	Alan Rufus Waters
JMAS	13	3	1975	469-81	G. N. Uzoigwe
Race	13	2	1971/72	251-2	Christopher Fyfe

204 Gordon, C. T.
THE GROWTH OF BOER OPPOSITION TO KRUGER, 1890-1895.
Cape Town, New York, Oxford University Press, 1970.

Hist	57	191	1972	474-5	R. Hyam
IJAHS	5	2	1972	307-9	Leslie Clement Duly
JAH	13	1	1972	160-1	T. R. H. Davenport

205 Graham, Sonia F.
GOVERNMENT AND MISSION EDUCATION IN NORTHERN NIGERIA, 1900-
1919, WITH SPECIAL REFERENCE TO THE WORK OF HANNS VISCHER.
WITH AN INTRODUCTION BY A. H. M. KIRK-GREENE.
Ibadan, Ibadan University Press, 1966.

Afr	42	2	1972	168-9	P. C. C. Evans
BSOAS	31	1	1968	211	D. W. Arnott
JAH	8	3	1967	550-1	R. E. Wraith

206 Gray, Sir John Milner
HISTORY OF ZANZIBAR, FROM THE MIDDLE AGES TO 1856.
London, Oxford University Press, 1962.

Afr	33	2	1963	160-1	John Middleton
Af Af	62	247	1963	166-7	Hilary Blood
AHR	68	4	1962/63	1140-1	Conrad C. Reining
BSOAS	26	3	1963	678	John E. Flint

Gray, Richard

(Gray, Sir John Milner)

EHR	79	313	1964	833-4	Eric Axelson
Hist	50	168	1965	131	J. E. Flint
JAH	4	2	1963	294-6	Roland Oliver

207   Gray, Richard
A HISTORY OF THE SOUTHERN SUDAN, 1839-1889.
London, Oxford University Press, 1961.

Af Af	61	245	1962	327-8	N. Barbour
AHR	68	1	1962/63	228-9	Garland G. Parker
BSOAS	25	2	1962	360-1	P. M. Holt
EHR	78	307	1963	404-6	H. S. Deighton
Hist	47	161	1962	346-7	George Bennett
JAH	4	1	1963	132-3	Margery Perham
Race	3	2	1961/62	81-2	D. A. Low

208   Gray, Richard
PRE-COLONIAL AFRICAN TRADE: ESSAYS ON TRADE IN CENTRAL AND
EASTERN AFRICA BEFORE 1900; EDITED BY RICHARD GRAY AND DAVID
BIRMINGHAM.
London, New York, Oxford U.P., 1970.

Afr	42	2	1972	172	R. G. Abrahams
Af Af	70	281	1971	410-1	David William Cohen
Af HS	4	2	1971	473-6	Gerald W. Hartwig
Af StR	13	2	1970	319-21	Melvin E. Page
AHR	76	2	1971	537	Margaret L. Bates
EHR	87	344	1972	622	John D. Hargreaves
Hist	56	187	1971	311	Cyril Ehrlich
JAH	11	4	1970	611-4	J. Vansina
JMAS	11	4	1973	662-4	Matthias A. Ogutu

209   Gray, Richard
THE TWO NATIONS; ASPECTS OF THE DEVELOPMENT OF RACE RELATIONS
IN THE RHODESIAS AND NYASALAND.
Issued under the auspices of the Institute of Race Relations,
London, New York, Oxford University Press, 1960.

Afr	31	4	1961	383	G. Beresford-Stooke
Af Af	60	238	1961	112-3	M. L. Clark
JAH	2	1	1961	164-6	J. D. Fage
RLJ	--	30	1961	56-8	R. Robinson

210 Greaves, Lionel Bruce
     CAREY FRANCIS OF KENYA.
     London, Rex Collings Ltd., 1969.

Af Af	70	281	1971	418-9	B. M.
JMAS	9	2	1971	333-5	Roger Van Zwanenberg
Race	12	3	1970/71	373-4	Sally Abbott

211 Greenberg, Joseph Harold
     THE LANGUAGES OF AFRICA.
     Bloomington, Indiana University, 1963.
     International Journal of American Linguistics, Part 2, Vol.
     XXIX, No. 1, 1963.

JAH	5	1	1964	135-6	Malcolm Guthrie

212 Greenfield, Richard
     ETHIOPIA; A NEW POLITICAL HISTORY.
     New York, F. A. Praeger, 1965.

AHR	71	4	1965/66	1400-1	Robert L. Hess
JMAS	3	4	1965	631-3	Michael F. Lofchie
Race	7	3	1965/66	313-5	Czesław Jeśman
Race	8	3	1966/67	303-4	Clyde Sanger

213 Gregory, Robert G.
     INDIA AND EAST AFRICA: A HISTORY OF RACE RELATIONS WITHIN
     THE BRITISH EMPIRE, 1890-1939.
     Oxford, Clarendon Press, 1971.

Af Af	72	286	1973	90	Karim K. Janmohamed
AHR	80	1	1975	115-6	Robert L. Tignor
EHR	89	350	1974	228-9	J. M. Brown
Hist	58	193	1973	328-9	John Lonsdale
IJAHS	5	3	1972	490-3	Harvey G. Soff
JAH	14	2	1973	347-9	Nizar A. Motani
JMAS	13	1	1975	172-3	T. G. Ramamurthi

214 Gregory, Robert G.
     SIDNEY WEBB AND EAST AFRICA; LABOUR'S EXPERIMENT WITH THE
     DOCTRINE OF NATIVE PARAMOUNTCY.
     Berkeley, University of California Press, 1962.

Afr	33	3	1963	275-6	George Bennett
Af Af	64	256	1965	226-8	H. B. Thomas

Greindl, Léopold

```
(Gregory, Robert G.)
AHR     68   4    1962/63   1141      Garland G. Parker
EHR     80   314  1965      214-5     John D. Hargreaves
Hist    48   163  1963      256       -----
```

215   Greindl, Léopold
      A LA RECHERCHE D'UN ÉTAT INDÉPENDANT: LÉOPOLD II ET LES
      PHILIPPINES (1869-1875).
      Bruxelles, 1962.

```
JAH     4    1    1963      138-40    Roger Anstey
```

216   Grenville, John Ashley Soames
      LORD SALISBURY AND FOREIGN POLICY: THE CLOSE OF THE NINETEENTH
      CENTURY.
      London, University of London, Athlone Press, 1964.

```
HJ      7    2    1964      340-4     Zara Steiner
JAH     7    2    1966      350-4     G. N. Sanderson
```

217   Grimal, Henri
      LA DÉCOLONISATION, 1919-1963.
      Paris, A. Colin, 1965.

```
AHR     71   4    1965/66   1295      S. C. Easton
JMAS    4    4    1966      549-51    Walter Markov
```

218   Groves, Charles Pelham
      THE PLANTING OF CHRISTIANITY IN AFRICA.
      VOL. 1.   TO 1840.
      VOL. 2.   1840-1878.
      VOL. 3.   1878-1914.
      VOL. 4.   1914-1954.
      London, Lutterworth Press, 1948-58.

Complete
```
JAH     1    1    1960      157-9     N. Q. King
```

Vol. 1
```
Afr     20   1    1950      84-5      Edwin W. Smith
```

Vol. 2
```
Afr     25   3    1955      297-8     Edwin W. Smith
```

Hailey, William Malcolm Hailey

(Groves, Charles Pelham)

<u>Vol. 3</u>

Afr	26	1	1956	86-8	Edwin W. Smith
Af Af	54	217	1955	327-8	Edwin W. Smith

<u>Vol. 4</u>

Afr	28	4	1958	372-4	Lyndon Harries

219 Grundy, Kenneth W.
CONFRONTATION AND ACCOMMODATION IN SOUTHERN AFRICA; THE LIMITS
OF INDEPENDENCE.
Berkeley, University of California Press, 1973.

Af StR	17	1	1974	280-2	Timothy M. Shaw
JMAS	12	4	1974	654-5	Timothy M. Shaw

220 Hahn, Carl Hugo Linsingen
THE NATIVE TRIBES OF SOUTH WEST AFRICA.
Cape Town, Cape Times Limited, 1928.

THE NATIVE TRIBES OF SOUTH WEST AFRICA, BY C. H. L. HAHN,
H. VEDDER AND L. FOURIE.
New York, Barnes and Noble, 1966.

Af Af	66	265	1967	377	N. E. Mustoe
JMAS	6	4	1968	600-3	Franz Ansprenger

221 Hailey, William Malcolm Hailey, baron
AN AFRICAN SURVEY; A STUDY OF PROBLEMS ARISING IN AFRICA SOUTH
OF THE SAHARA. REVISED 1956.
London, New York, Oxford University Press, 1957.

Afr	28	2	1958	168-70	Edwin W. Smith
Af Af	56	225	1957	325-7	Alan Grey

222 Hailey, William Malcolm Hailey, baron
NATIVE ADMINISTRATION IN THE BRITISH TERRITORIES IN AFRICA.
4 VOLS.
London, H. M. Stationery Office, 1951.

NATIVE ADMINISTRATION IN THE BRITISH AFRICAN TERRITORIES.
PT. 1.   EAST AFRICA: UGANDA, KENYA, TANGANYIKA.
PT. 2.   CENTRAL AFRICA: ZANZIBAR, NYASALAND, NORTHERN
          RHODESIA.

Hall, Richard Seymour

(Hailey, William Malcolm Hailey, baron)
PT. 3. WEST AFRICA: NIGERIA, GOLD COAST, SIERRA LEONE,
        GAMBIA.
PT. 4. A GENERAL SURVEY OF THE SYSTEM OF NATIVE ADMINISTRA-
        TION.
PT. 5. THE HIGH COMMISSION TERRITORIES: BASUTOLAND, THE
        BECHUANALAND PROTECTORATE AND SWAZILAND.
London, H. M. Stationery Office, 1950-3.

Pt. 1-4					
Afr	21	4	1951	336-9	L. P. Mair

Pt. 5					
Afr	24	2	1954	168-9	L. P. Mair
Af Af	52	209	1953	341-2	A. Sillery

223   Hall, Richard Seymour
      ZAMBIA.
      New York, Praeger, 1966 (c1965).
      London, Pall Mall Press, 1965.

AHR	72	1	1966/67	257	Colin Rhys Lovell
JMAS	5	3	1967	432-3	Otakar Hulec
Race	7	4	1965/66	422-4	Robert I. Rotberg

224   Hallett, Robin
      AFRICA SINCE 1875; A MODERN HISTORY.
      Ann Arbor, University of Michigan Press, 1974.

Af StR	18	2	1975	134-9	Nizar A. Motani
IJAHS	8	3	1975	493-6	Robert W. July
JMAS	13	2	1975	358-60	Erving E. Beauregard

225   Hallett, Robin
      AFRICA TO 1875; A MODERN HISTORY.
      Ann Arbor, University of Michigan Press, 1970.

Af HS	4	1	1971	165-6	Norman R. Bennett
AHR	76	1	1971	177-8	Donald L. Wiedner
JAH	11	4	1970	605-6	John D. Hargreaves
JMAS	9	2	1971	312-5	Erving E. Beauregard

226   Hallett, Robin
      THE PENETRATION OF AFRICA; EUROPEAN ENTERPRISE AND EXPLORATION
      PRINCIPALLY IN NORTHERN AND WESTERN AFRICA UP TO 1830.

Hancock, William Keith

(Hallett, Robin)
VOL. 1. TO 1815.
London, Routledge and K. Paul, 1965- .

THE PENETRATION OF AFRICA; EUROPEAN EXPLORATION IN NORTH AND
WEST AFRICA TO 1815.
New York, Praeger, 1965.

AHR	71	4	1965/66	1398-9	H. S. Wilson
EHR	82	323	1967	412	John D. Hargreaves
JAH	8	1	1967	166-7	J. D. Fage

227 Halpern, Jack
SOUTH AFRICA'S HOSTAGES: BASUTOLAND, BECHUANALAND AND SWAZI-
LAND.
Baltimore, Penguin Books, 1965.

JMAS	4	1	1966	119	E. L. Muth
JMAS	5	4	1967	541-55	J. E. Spence
Race	8	2	1966/67	198-200	J. E. Spence

228 Hammond, Richard James
PORTUGAL AND AFRICA, 1815-1910; A STUDY IN UNECONOMIC IMPERI-
ALISM.
Stanford, Stanford University Press, 1966.

Af Af	67	266	1968	77-8	Mabel Jackson Haight
Af St	27	2	1968	102-3	J. L. R. Torres
AHR	72	3	1966/67	1050-1	J. R. Hooker
EHR	83	329	1968	862	C. R. Boxer
JAH	9	1	1968	168-70	Douglas L. Wheeler
JMAS	7	3	1969	544-6	Edward A. Alpers
Race	9	2	1967/68	265-7	C. R. Boxer

229 Hancock, William Keith
SMUTS.
VOL. 1. THE SANGUINE YEARS, 1870-1919.
VOL. 2. THE FIELDS OF FORCE, 1919-1950.
Cambridge, University Press, 1962-8.

Vol. 1

Af Af	62	246	1963	75-6	Marjorie Juta
AHR	68	4	1962/63	1068-70	George Curry
EHR	79	313	1964	803-5	A. F. McC. Madden
HJ	11	2	1968	565-81	Eric A. Walker

Hanna, Alexander John

    (Hancock, William Keith)

Hist	48	163	1963	255-6	J. L. McCracken
JAH	4	2	1963	289-90	Eric Stokes

    Vol. 2

Af Af	67	268	1968	271-4	D. M. van der H. Schreuder
Af HS	1	2	1968	280-4	Jeffrey Butler
AHR	74	3	1968/69	1059-60	James L. Godfrey
EHR	84	333	1969	879-80	A. F. McC. Madden
HJ	11	2	1968	565-81	Eric A. Walker
Hist	54	180	1969	153-4	J. L. McCracken
JAH	9	3	1968	491-4	Roland Oliver

230   Hanna, Alexander John
    THE BEGINNINGS OF NYASALAND AND NORTH-EASTERN RHODESIA,
    1859-95.
    Oxford, Clarendon Press, 1956.

Afr	26	3	1956	306-9	J. A. Barnes
Af Af	55	219	1956	154-5	George Craig
EHR	72	282	1957	194-5	George Shepperson

231   Hanna, Alexander John
    THE STORY OF THE RHODESIAS AND NYASALAND.
    London, Faber and Faber, 1960.

Af Af	60	238	1961	111-2	D. Lombard
Af Af	64	257	1965	297-8	Claude A. Collard
EHR	77	302	1962	194-5	George Shepperson
Hist	46	157	1961	182	J. D. Hargreaves
JAH	2	1	1961	162-4	Richard Gray

232   Harbeson, John Willis
    NATION-BUILDING IN KENYA; THE ROLE OF LAND REFORM.
    Evanston, Northwestern University Press, 1973.

JAH	15	1	1974	165-6	Frank Furedi
JMAS	11	3	1973	481-4	E. Philip Morgan

233   Hargreaves, John D.
    A LIFE OF SIR SAMUEL LEWIS.
    London, Oxford University Press, 1958.

Afr	29	2	1959	207-8	Michael Banton
Af Af	58	233	1959	340-1	Harry Sawyer

```
(Hargreaves, John D.)
AHR      64   1    1958/59   79-80    Garland G. Parker
BSOAS    22   1    1959      198      A. N. Allott
EHR      74   291  1959      370      Freda Wolfson
Hist     44   150  1959      92-3     George Bennett
JAH      1    1    1960      170-1    J. F. Ade Ajayi
```

234   Hargreaves, John D.
       PRELUDE TO THE PARTITION OF WEST AFRICA.
       London, Macmillan; New York, St. Martin's Press, 1963.

```
Afr      34   2    1964      182-3    C. W. Newbury
Af Af    63   251  1964      147-8    C. W. Newbury
AHR      69   4    1963/64   1065-6   Arthur N. Cook
EHR      80   316  1965      630-1    Freda Harcourt
HJ       7    1    1964      154-69   Ronald Hyam
Hist     50   168  1965      134-6    Kenneth Robinson
JAH      5    1    1964      121-5    Henri Brunschwig
JMAS     1    4    1963      557-8    Saadia Touval
```

235   Hargreaves, John D.
       WEST AFRICA: THE FORMER FRENCH STATES.
       Englewood Cliffs, N. J., Prentice-Hall, 1967.

```
Afr      37   4    1967      488      Hubert Deschamps
Af Af    67   268  1968      265-6    C. W. Newbury
Af HS    2    1    1969      147-9    Roger Pasquier
AHR      73   2    1967/68   560      George E. Brooks, Jr.
Hist     54   180  1969      152-3    A. G. Hopkins
JAH      9    1    1968      160-1    Robert R. Griffith
```

236   Hargreaves, John D.
       WEST AFRICA PARTITIONED.
       VOL. 1. THE LOADED PAUSE, 1885-1889.
       Madison, University of Wisconsin Press, 1974- .

```
IJAHS    8    4    1975      705-7    John Flint
```

237   Harris, Brice
       THE UNITED STATES AND THE ITALO-ETHIOPIAN CRISIS.
       Stanford, Stanford University Press, 1964.

```
Af Af    64   247  1965      314      -----
AHR      71   1    1965/66   117-8    S. Adler
```

Hatch, John Charles

(Harris, Brice)
| EHR | 82 | 322 | 1967 | 205-6 | Edward Ullendorff |
| JMAS | 3 | 2 | 1965 | 312-4 | Richard Pankhurst |

238   Hatch, John Charles
THE HISTORY OF BRITAIN IN AFRICA FROM THE FIFTEENTH CENTURY TO
THE PRESENT.
London, Deutsch, 1969.
New York, Praeger, 1969.

Afr	41	1	1971	72-3	Hubert Deschamps
Af Af	69	277	1970	399-400	W. P. Kirkman
Af HS	3	2	1970	476	Harrison Wright

239   Heggoy, Alf Andrew
THE AFRICAN POLICIES OF GABRIEL HANOTAUX, 1894-1898.
Athens, University of Georgia Press, 1972.

AHR	80	1	1975	127	Erving E. Beauregard
IJAHS	6	2	1973	344-6	A. S. Kanya-Forstner
JAH	13	4	1972	704	John D. Hargreaves

240   Herd, Norman
1922: THE REVOLT ON THE RAND.
Johannesburg, Blue Crane Books, 1966.

| Af HS | 1 | 1 | 1968 | 108 | William H. Friedland |
| JMAS | 6 | 4 | 1968 | 594 | Erving E. Beauregard |

241   Herskovits, Melville Jean
DAHOMEAN NARRATIVE; A CROSS-CULTURAL ANALYSIS, BY MELVILLE J.
HERSKOVITS AND FRANCES S. HERSKOVITS.
Evanston, Northwestern University Press, 1958.

| Afr | 29 | 3 | 1959 | 311-3 | W. R. G. Horton |
| Af St | 19 | 2 | 1960 | 107-10 | G. F. |

242   Herskovits, Melville Jean
THE HUMAN FACTOR IN CHANGING AFRICA.
London, Routledge and K. Paul, 1962.
New York, Knopf, 1962.

| JMAS | 1 | 4 | 1963 | 555-7 | John Hatch |

243   Hertefelt, Marcel D'
       LES CLANS DU RWANDA ANCIEN. ÉLÉMENTS D'ETHNOSOCIOLOGIE ET
       D'ETHNOHISTOIRE.
       Tervuren, Musée royal de l'Afrique centrale, 1971.

Afr	42	4	1972	353-4	Jacques Maquet
Af StR	17	2	1974	467-72	David William Cohen

244   Hess, Robert L.
       ETHIOPIA; THE MODERNIZATION OF AUTOCRACY.
       Ithaca, Cornell University Press, 1970.

Af HS	4	1	1971	166-8	Herbert S. Lewis
Af StR	14	1	1971	167-8	Simon D. Messing
AHR	76	4	1971	1203	Alessandro Triulzi
JAH	12	3	1971	501-3	P. S. Gilkes
JMAS	9	3	1971	498-505	James C. N. Paul

245   Hess, Robert L.
       ITALIAN COLONIALISM IN SOMALIA.
       Chicago, University of Chicago Press, 1966.

Afr	38	3	1968	354-5	V. Luling
AHR	72	4	1966/67	1456-7	Harold G. Marcus
EHR	83	328	1968	637	B. W. Andrzejewski
JAH	8	3	1967	553-4	I. M. Lewis
JMAS	6	2	1968	284-6	Leone Iraci
Race	9	1	1967/68	118	I. M. Lewis

246   Heusch, Luc de, comp.
       LE ROI IVRE; OU, L'ORIGINE DE L'ÉTAT; MYTHES ET RITES BANTOUS.
       Paris, Gallimard, 1972.

Afr	43	4	1973	379-80	Jan Vansina
JAH	15	1	1974	131-5	C. C. Wrigley

247   Heussler, Robert
       THE BRITISH IN NORTHERN NIGERIA.
       London, New York, Oxford University Press, 1968.

Afr	39	3	1969	320-1	P. C. Lloyd
Af Af	70	279	1971	187	Rex Niven
Af HS	3	1	1970	221-5	D. J. M. Muffett
AHR	75	2	1969/70	556	L. Gray Cowan

Heussler, Robert

(Heussler, Robert)

BSOAS	32	2	1969	444–5	Mervyn Hiskett
EHR	86	338	1971	195–6	P. E. H. Hair
Hist	54	182	1969	465	A. J. H. Latham
JAH	10	2	1969	328–9	David Craig Dorward
JMAS	7	4	1969	756–8	John A. Ballard
Race	11	3	1969/70	380–1	Philip Mason

248   Heussler, Robert
YESTERDAY'S RULERS; THE MAKING OF THE BRITISH COLONIAL SERVICE.
FOREWORD BY JOHN MACPHERSON.   INTROD. BY MARGERY PERHAM.
Syracuse, N. Y., Syracuse University Press, 1963.

Afr	34	2	1964	181–2	George Bennett
Af Af	63	251	1964	146–7	Hilary Blood
AHR	68	4	1962/63	1036–7	H. Duncan Hall
JMAS	1	4	1963	558–60	Alec Dickson
Race	5	3	1963/64	73–4	John Gullick

249   Hill, Richard Leslie
EGYPT IN THE SUDAN, 1820–1881.
London, New York, Oxford University Press, 1959.

AHR	64	4	1958/59	980	C. Ernest Dawn
BSOAS	24	1	1961	172	-----
EHR	75	296	1960	541	A. H. Hourani
Hist	46	157	1961	178–80	G. N. Sanderson
JAH	1	1	1960	168–70	Richard Gray

250   HISTORY OF EAST AFRICA, EDITED BY ROLAND OLIVER AND OTHERS.
Oxford, Clarendon Press, 1963-   .

Vol. 1

Afr	34	2	1964	177–80	John Middleton
Af Af	63	250	1964	77–80	Mona Macmillan
Af St	24	2	1965	122–4	N. G. Garson
AHR	69	2	1963/64	531	Marvin G. Pursinger
BSOAS	27	1	1964	206–8	Kenneth Ingham
EHR	80	314	1965	125–8	George Bennett
Hist	50	168	1965	130	George Shepperson
JAH	5	2	1964	299–304	C. C. Wrigley
Race	6	2	1964/65	159–62	Richard Gray
RLJ	--	35	1964	81–4	Merrick Posnansky

Hogben, Sidney John

(HISTORY OF EAST AFRICA)

Vol. 2

Af Af	65	260	1966	259-60	Arthur Kirby
Af SR	--	3	1967	237-8	J. D. Omer-Cooper
AHR	71	4	1965/66	1401-2	Robert I. Rotberg
BSOAS	29	3	1966	659-60	Shula Marks
EHR	82	325	1967	870-1	George Shepperson
Hist	52	176	1967	375-6	A. J. Hanna
Race	7	4	1965/66	420-1	Richard Gray

251   A HISTORY OF TANZANIA. EDITED BY I. N. KIMAMBO AND A. J. TEMU. Nairobi, published for the Historical Association of Tanzania by the East African Pub. House, 1969.

Afr	41	1	1971	82	-----
Af SR	--	12	1971	149-51	E. R. Turton

252   Hodgkin, Thomas Lionel
AFRICAN POLITICAL PARTIES, AN INTRODUCTORY GUIDE.
Harmondsworth, Middlesex, Penguin Books, 1962 (c1961).

Afr	32	3	1962	293	P. C. Lloyd

253   Hodgkin, Thomas Lionel
NATIONALISM IN COLONIAL AFRICA.
London, Muller, 1956.
New York, New York University Press, 1957.

Afr	27	4	1957	413-4	L. P. Mair
Af St	16	1	1957	72	Julius Lewin
AHR	64	1	1958/59	141-2	Charles B. Realey
BSOAS	19	3	1957	623-4	D. H. Jones

254   Hogben, Sidney John
THE EMIRATES OF NORTHERN NIGERIA; A PRELIMINARY SURVEY OF THEIR HISTORICAL TRADITIONS, BY S. J. HOGBEN AND A. H. M. KIRK-GREENE.
London, Oxford University Press, 1966.

Afr	37	2	1967	229-30	M. G. Smith
Af Af	66	264	1967	262-4	K. W. J. Post
BSOAS	30	1	1967	232-4	M. Hiskett
EHR	83	330	1967	134-6	J. O. Hunwick

Holden, Edith

(Hogben, Sidney John)
Hist	54	180	1969	148	Christopher Fyfe
JAH	7	3	1966	520-2	D. H. Jones
Race	8	1	1966/67	104	Colin Newbury

255   Holden, Edith
BLYDEN OF LIBERIA; AN ACCOUNT OF THE LIFE AND LABORS OF EDWARD
WILMOT BLYDEN, LL.D., AS RECORDED IN LETTERS AND IN PRINT.
FOREWORD BY NNAMDI AZIKIWE.
New York, Vantage Press, 1967 (c1966).

Af Af	67	266	1968	70-2	Richard Symonds
Af HS	1	2	1968	294-6	Christopher Fyfe
JAH	9	1	1968	174-6	Hollis R. Lynch
JMAS	5	3	1967	433-5	P. E. H. Hair

256   Hollingsworth, Lawrence William
ZANZIBAR UNDER THE FOREIGN OFFICE, 1890-1913.
London, Macmillan, 1953.

Afr	26	3	1956	306	L. P. Mair
Af Af	52	208	1953	253-4	R. A. Oliver
BSOAS	18	2	1956	397	R. A. Hamilton
Hist	38	132	1953	93	-----

257   Holmberg, Åke
AFRICAN TRIBES AND EUROPEAN AGENCIES. COLONIALISM AND HUMAN-
ITARIANISM IN BRITISH SOUTH AND EAST AFRICA 1870-1895.
Göteborg, Akademiförlaget, 1966.

Af Af	67	269	1968	355-7	Jeffrey Butler
Af HS	2	1	1969	151-2	Carl Haywood
AHR	72	4	1966/67	1457-8	Colin Rhys Lovell
EHR	82	325	1967	866-7	A. Sillery
Hist	53	178	1968	300	George Shepperson
JAH	8	2	1967	357-9	Richard Brown

258   Holt, Peter Malcolm
THE MAHDIST STATE IN THE SUDAN, 1881-1898; A STUDY OF ITS
ORIGINS, DEVELOPMENT AND OVERTHROW.
Oxford, Clarendon Press, 1958.

Afr	29	3	1959	319-20	I. Cunnison
Af Af	58	231	1959	185-6	S. S.

Houghton, D. Hobart

(Holt, Peter Malcolm)

AHR	64	3	1958/59	717	Sydney Nettleton Fisher
BSOAS	22	1	1959	146-7	R. B. Serjeant
EHR	75	296	1960	551	J. W. Crowfoot
Hist	46	157	1961	178-80	G. N. Sanderson
IJAHS	5	2	1972	306-7	John Voll

259   Holt, Peter Malcolm
A MODERN HISTORY OF THE SUDAN, FROM THE FUNJ SULTANATE TO THE
PRESENT DAY.
London, Weidenfeld and Nicolson, 1961.

BSOAS	25	2	1962	359-60	A. H. Hourani
EHR	78	306	1963	166-7	H. S. Deighton
Hist	47	160	1962	211	A. J. Arkell
JAH	3	1	1962	143-4	P. L. Shinnie

260   Hopkins, Anthony G.
AN ECONOMIC HISTORY OF WEST AFRICA.
London, Longman, 1973.
New York, Columbia University Press, 1973.

Afr	45	2	1975	214-5	Rowena M. Lawson
Af Af	73	291	1974	236-7	Paul E. Lovejoy
Af StR	17	1	1974	277-80	Ralph A. Austen
AHR	80	2	1975	447-8	George E. Brooks
BSOAS	38	1	1975	201-2	Richard Rathbone
Hist	59	196	1974	305-6	A. J. H. Latham
IJAHS	7	3	1974	540-3	Philip D. Curtin
JAH	15	2	1974	323-5	C. C. Wrigley

261   Hoskyns, Catherine
THE CONGO SINCE INDEPENDENCE, JANUARY 1960-DECEMBER 1961.
London, New York, Oxford University Press, 1965.

Af Af	64	255	1965	129-30	E. M.
AHR	71	1	1965/66	269-70	D. L. Wiedner
JMAS	4	1	1966	111-5	Colin Legum
Race	7	1	1965/66	91-2	Claude Welch

262   Houghton, D. Hobart
THE SOUTH AFRICAN ECONOMY.
Cape Town, New York, Oxford University Press, 1964; 2d ed.,
1967.

Huberich, Charles Henry

    (Houghton, D. Hobart)
    Af Af   63   253   1964   308   -----

    2d ed.
    Af Af   68   270   1969   71-2   W. E.

263   Huberich, Charles Henry
    THE POLITICAL AND LEGISLATIVE HISTORY OF LIBERIA; A DOCUMENTARY
    HISTORY OF THE CONSTITUTIONS, LAWS AND TREATIES OF LIBERIA FROM
    THE EARLIEST SETTLEMENTS TO THE ESTABLISHMENT OF THE REPUBLIC,
    A SKETCH OF THE ACTIVITIES OF THE AMERICAN COLONIZATION SOCI-
    ETIES, A COMMENTARY ON THE CONSTITUTION OF THE REPUBLIC AND A
    SURVEY OF THE POLITICAL AND SOCIAL LEGISLATION FROM 1847 TO
    1944; WITH APPENDICES CONTAINING THE LAWS OF THE COLONY OF
    LIBERIA, 1820-1839, AND ACTS OF THE GOVERNOR AND COUNCIL,
    1839-1847. FOREWORD BY ROSCOE POUND.
    New York, Central Book Co., 1947.

    Afr   19 1   1949   78-9   H. G. A. Hughes

264   Hunter, Guy, ed.
    INDUSTRIALISATION AND RACE RELATIONS; A SYMPOSIUM.
    London, New York, Oxford University Press, 1965.

    Af Af   65 258 1966   103-4   J. P. M.
    JMAS   4   3   1966   391-3   Ralph E. S. Tanner
    Race   7   3   1965/66 303-4   Tom Soper

265   Hunter, Guy
    THE NEW SOCIETIES OF TROPICAL AFRICA; A SELECTIVE STUDY.
    London, New York, Oxford University Press, 1962.
    New York, Praeger, 1964 (c1962).

    Afr   33 1   1963   75   P. C. Lloyd
    Af Af   62 246 1963   82-3   Peter C. W. Gutkind
    BSOAS 26 2   1963   474-5   A. Cohen
    JAH   4   2   1963   307-8   Gustav Jahoda
    JMAS   1   2   1963   267-70   Theodore Bull
    RLJ   -- 32   1962   52-3   C. M. N. White

266   Huttenback, Robert A.
    GANDHI IN SOUTH AFRICA; BRITISH IMPERIALISM AND THE INDIAN
    QUESTION, 1860-1914.
    Ithaca, Cornell University Press, 1971.

Iliffe, John

(Huttenback, Robert A.)
```
Af HS    4    2    1971    460-2    J. S. Mangat
AHR     77    3    1972    745      Ainslie T. Embree
JAH     14    3    1973    523-7    Hugh Tinker
```

267   Hyam, Roland
THE FAILURE OF SOUTH AFRICAN EXPANSION, 1908-1948.
London, Macmillan, 1972.
New York, Africana Pub. Corp., 1972.

```
Af Af    72    289    1973    458-9    Martin Legassick
EHR      89    351    1974    464      A. Sillery
Hist     59    196    1974    313-4    Shula Marks
IJAHS     6      4    1973    685-8    Lewis H. Gann
JAH      14      3    1973    522-3    J. E. Spence
JMAS     12      3    1974    512-3    C. W. de Kiewiet
```

268   Ikime, Obaro
MERCHANT PRINCE OF THE NIGER DELTA: THE RISE AND FALL OF
NANA OLOMU, LAST GOVERNOR OF THE BENIN RIVER.
London, Ibadan, Heinemann Educational, 1968.
New York, Africana Pub. Corp., 1969 (c1968).

```
Hist     55    183    1970    154      Cyril Ehrlich
IJAHS     5      3    1972    493-4    K. O. Diké
```

269   Ikime, Obaro
NIGER DELTA RIVALRY: ITSEKIRI-URHOBO RELATIONS AND THE
EUROPEAN PRESENCE, 1884-1936.
Harlow, Longmans, 1969.
New York, Humanities Press, 1969.

```
Afr      43    1    1973    78-80     G. I. Jones
Af Af    71    282   1972    92-3      Elizabeth Isichei
Af HS     4    1    1971    157-60    G. I. Jones
Af StR   15    1    1972    139-45    David Northrup
AHR      76    2    1971    535-6     J. E. Flint
BSOAS    34    2    1971    447-8     P. C. Lloyd
JAH      16    2    1975    308-9     D. H. Jones
```

270   Iliffe, John
TANGANYIKA UNDER GERMAN RULE, 1905-1912.
London, Cambridge U.P., 1969.
Nairobi, East African Pub. House, 1969.

Ingham, Kenneth

(Iliffe, John)

Afr	41	2	1971	169-70	R. G. Abrahams
Af HS	2	2	1969	366-7	Norman R. Bennett
Af St	29	4	1970	307-8	Noam J. Pines
Af StR	13	2	1970	315-6	Terry H. Elkiss
AHR	75	4	1969/70	1166-8	J. Gus Liebenow
Hist	57	189	1972	156-7	G. N. Sanderson
JAH	10	3	1969	499-501	Marcia Wright
Race	11	2	1969/70	254-6	J. A. Kieran

271 Ingham, Kenneth
A HISTORY OF EAST AFRICA.
New York, Praeger, 1962.

Af Af	61	245	1962	354	-----
EHR	79	310	1964	199-200	George Bennett
JAH	4	2	1963	292-3	C. C. Wrigley

272 Ingham, Kenneth
THE MAKING OF MODERN UGANDA.
London, Allen and Unwin, 1958.

Afr	29	2	1959	205	John Beattie
Af Af	57	228	1958	243-4	H. B. Thomas
EHR	74	291	1959	376	George Shepperson
Hist	44	150	1959	93	Leslie Uganda
JAH	1	1	1960	163-6	Roland Oliver

273 International African Seminar. 1st, Kampala, Uganda, 1959.
SOCIAL CHANGE IN MODERN AFRICA; STUDIES PRESENTED AND DIS-
CUSSED. EDITED BY AIDAN SOUTHALL. FOREWORD BY DARYLL FORDE.
London, New York, published for the International African In-
stitute by the Oxford University Press, 1961.

Af Af	61	242	1962	76-7	Lucy Mair

274 International African Seminar. 4th, Dakar, Senegal, 1961.
THE HISTORIAN IN TROPICAL AFRICA; STUDIES PRESENTED AND DIS-
CUSSED. EDITED WITH AN INTROD. BY J. VANSINA, R. MAUNY, AND
L. V. THOMAS.
London, published for the International African Institute by
the Oxford University Press, 1964.

Af Af	63	253	1964	299-301	Hilary Blood
Af St	24	2	1965	122-4	N. G. Garson

Isaacman, Allen F.

(International African Seminar)

AHR	70	3	1964/65	785-6	Peter Duignan
BSOAS	28	1	1965	197	D. H. Jones
Hist	51	171	1966	129-30	George Shepperson
JAH	6	2	1965	233-5	Eric Stokes
RLJ	--	37	1967	63-5	Robert I. Rotberg

275   International African Seminar. 5th, Zaria, Nigeria, 1964.
ISLAM IN TROPICAL AFRICA: STUDIES PRESENTED AND DISCUSSED AT
THE FIFTH INTERNATIONAL AFRICAN SEMINAR, AHMADU BELLO UNIVER-
SITY, ZARIA, JANUARY 1964; EDITED WITH AN INTRODUCTION BY
I. M. LEWIS, FOREWORD BY DARYLL FORDE.
London, published for the International African Institute by
the Oxford University Press, 1966.

Af Af	67	267	1968	159-60	A. S. Bujra
BSOAS	31	2	1968	437-40	Humphrey J. Fisher
JAH	8	3	1967	558-60	W. Montgomery Watt
JMAS	5	4	1967	596-7	Charles O. Cecil

276   International African Seminar. 7th, University of Ghana,
1965.
CHRISTIANITY IN TROPICAL AFRICA: STUDIES PRESENTED AND DIS-
CUSSED AT THE SEVENTH INTERNATIONAL AFRICAN SEMINAR, UNIVERSITY
OF GHANA, APRIL 1965; EDITED WITH AN INTRODUCTION BY C. G.
BAËTA, FOREWORD BY DARYLL FORDE.
London, published for the International African Institute by
the Oxford University Press, 1968.

Afr	39	1	1969	95-6	H. W. Turner
Af Af	67	268	1968	254-6	Aylward Shorter W. F.
Af St	32	1	1973	55-6	A. G. Schutte
BSOAS	32	1	1969	211-3	Humphrey J. Fisher
JAH	10	2	1969	336-40	E. A. Ayandele

277   Isaacman, Allen F.
MOZAMBIQUE: THE AFRICANIZATION OF A EUROPEAN INSTITUTION;
THE ZAMBESI PRAZOS, 1750-1902.
Madison, University of Wisconsin Press, 1972.

Af Af	73	292	1974	372-4	David Birmingham
Af StR	16	1	1973	133-4	Thomas H. Henriksen
AHR	80	4	1975	1023	Donald L. Wiedner
BSOAS	36	3	1973	727-8	Richard Gray
Hist	60	199	1975	252	John Lonsdale

Itote, Waruhiu

(Isaacman, Allen F.)
IJAHS	6	1	1973	136-7	Douglas L. Wheeler
JAH	14	2	1973	340-2	Gerhard Liesegang
JMAS	12	3	1974	487-91	Walter C. Opello, Jr.

278   Itote, Waruhiu
"MAU MAU" GENERAL.
Nairobi, East African Institute Press, 1967.

JAH	9	1	1968	179-80	George Bennett

279   Jahoda, Gustav
WHITE MAN; A STUDY OF THE ATTITUDES OF AFRICANS TO EUROPEANS
IN GHANA BEFORE INDEPENDENCE.
London, New York, Oxford University Press, 1961.

Afr	31	4	1961	390-1	Michael Banton
Af Af	61	243	1962	166-7	Iain Gunn
BSOAS	25	3	1962	657-8	M. Guthrie
RLJ	--	30	1961	59-60	A. D. Jones

280   Jeśman, Czesław
THE ETHIOPIAN PARADOX.
Issued under the auspices of the Institute of Race Relations,
London, New York, Oxford University Press, 1963.

Afr	34	1	1964	66-7	Robert Hetzron
Af Af	63	253	1964	312	------
JMAS	1	3	1963	308-9	Graham Tayar
Race	5	3	1963/64	78	Norman Bentwich

281   Johnson, Willard R.
THE CAMEROON FEDERATION; POLITICAL INTEGRATION IN A FRAGMENTARY
SOCIETY.
Princeton, Princeton University Press, 1970.

Af Af	72	289	1973	453-4	J. F. Bayart
Af HS	4	1	1971	203-6	David E. Gardinier
Af SR	--	13	1972	229-31	Douglas G. Anglin
JMAS	11	2	1973	326-9	W. Norman Haupt

282   Johnston, Hugh Anthony Stephens
THE FULANI EMPIRE OF SOKOTO.
London, Ibadan, Oxford U.P., 1967.

July, Robert William

(Johnston, Hugh Anthony Stephens)

Afr	39	1	1969	78-9	M. G. Smith
Af Af	67	268	1968	267-9	Anthony Kirk-Greene
AHR	74	1	1968/69	243-4	Daniel F. McCall
BSOAS	32	3	1969	655-6	D. H. Jones
EHR	84	332	1969	635-6	John D. Hargreaves
Hist	54	180	1969	146-7	Humphrey Fisher
JAH	10	3	1969	490-3	John Ralph Willis

283   Jones, Griffith Bevan
BRITAIN AND NYASALAND.
London, Allen and Unwin, 1964.

Af Af	63	253	1964	291-2	Claude A. Collard
JAH	6	1	1965	131	George Shepperson
Race	7	4	1965/66	422-4	Robert I. Rotberg

284   Jones, Gwilym Iwan
THE TRADING STATES OF THE OIL RIVERS; A STUDY OF POLITICAL
DEVELOPMENT IN EASTERN NIGERIA.
London, published for the International African Institute by
Oxford University Press, 1963.

Afr	34	2	1964	175-6	P. C. Lloyd
Af Af	63	251	1964	153-4	Mercedes Mackay
AHR	69	4	1963/64	1152-3	Margaret L. Bates
EHR	80	315	1965	425	John D. Hargreaves
Hist	49	166	1964	273-4	Christopher Fyfe
JMAS	4	3	1966	349-57	Robert L. Tignor

285   July, Robert William
A HISTORY OF THE AFRICAN PEOPLE.
New York, Scribner, 1970.

Afr	41	1	1971	71-2	Robert Smith
Af Af	70	280	1971	309-10	E. O'Connor
Af HS	4	2	1971	465	Norman R. Bennett
BSOAS	35	1	1972	185-7	Shula Marks

286   July, Robert William
THE ORIGINS OF MODERN AFRICAN THOUGHT: ITS DEVELOPMENT IN
WEST AFRICA DURING THE NINETEENTH AND TWENTIETH CENTURIES.
London, Faber, 1968.
New York, F. A. Praeger, 1968 (c1967).

Kadalie, Clements

(July, Robert William)

Af Af	67	269	1968	354-5	J. S. Spiegler
Af HS	1	2	1968	284-5	John D. Hargreaves
AHR	74	2	1968/69	683-4	Philip D. Curtin
JAH	9	3	1968	488-9	Hollis R. Lynch
JMAS	6	4	1968	583-6	Abiola Irele

287   Kadalie, Clements
       MY LIFE AND THE ICU: THE AUTOBIOGRAPHY OF A BLACK TRADE
       UNIONIST IN SOUTH AFRICA; EDITED, WITH AN INTRODUCTION BY
       STANLEY TRAPIDO.
       London, Cass, 1970.
       New York, Humanities Press, 1970.

Af Af	70	280	1971	314	Sylvia Neame
Af HS	4	1	1971	206-11	Laurence Salomon
JAH	14	1	1973	159-61	George Shepperson
Race	12	3	1970/71	377-9	Brian Bunting

288   Kanya-Forstner, Alexander Sydney
       THE CONQUEST OF THE WESTERN SUDAN--A STUDY IN FRENCH MILITARY
       IMPERIALISM.
       London, Cambridge U.P., 1969.

Afr	40	2	1970	176	Hubert Deschamps
Af Af	70	279	1971	183-5	John D. Hargreaves
Af HS	3	1	1970	215-6	Martin Klein
AHR	75	6	1969/70	1755-6	Robert L. Tignor
BSOAS	35	1	1972	212-3	D. H. Jones
EHR	86	340	1971	638-9	P. E. H. Hair
JAH	13	5	1972	507-10	Yves Person
Race	12	1	1970/71	112-3	D. H. Jones

289   Kanza, Thomas R.
       CONFLICT IN THE CONGO: THE RISE AND FALL OF LUMUMBA, TRANS-
       LATED FROM THE FRENCH.
       Harmondsworth, Penguin, 1972.

Af Af	72	289	1973	457	Philip Whitaker
IJAHS	5	4	1972	686-7	Charles H. Stuart
JMAS	11	4	1973	649-53	Stephen R. Weissman

290   Karugire, Samwiri Rubaraza
       A HISTORY OF THE KINGDOM OF NKORE IN WESTERN UGANDA TO 1896.
       Oxford, Clarendon Press, 1971.

(Karugire, Samwiri Rubaraza)

Af Af	72	286	1973	89	Christopher Wrigley
BSOAS	36	3	1973	723-4	H. F. Morris
EHR	88	346	1973	200-1	Kenneth Ingham
IJAHS	5	3	1972	532-3	Edward I. Steinhart
JAH	14	1	1973	139-41	Jan Vansina

291   Katzenellenbogen, S. E.
RAILWAYS AND THE COPPER MINES OF KATANGA.
Oxford, Clarendon Press, 1973.

BSOAS	38	1	1975	203-4	A. D. Roberts
Hist	60	199	1975	255	Roger T. Anstey
IJAHS	8	1	1975	167-8	Jacques Louis Hymans

292   Kaunda, Kenneth David
ZAMBIA SHALL BE FREE; AN AUTOBIOGRAPHY.
London, Heinemann, 1962.
New York, Praeger, 1963 (c1962).

JMAS	1	3	1963	421-3	J. G. Markham

293   Kedourie, Elie
NATIONALISM IN ASIA AND AFRICA. EDITED AND WITH AN INTRODUC-
TION BY ELIE KEDOURIE.
New York, World Pub. Co., 1970.

JAH	14	1	1973	167-8	M. A. Cook
JMAS	10	4	1972	645-8	L. Adele Jinadu

294   Kent, Raymond K.
EARLY KINGDOMS IN MADAGASCAR, 1500-1700.
New York, Holt, Rinehart and Winston, 1970.

AHR	77	3	1972	823-4	N. R. Bennett
IJAHS	5	2	1972	280-1	Garland Downum
JAH	13	1	1972	151-2	Hubert Deschamps

295   Kerr, Alexander
FORT HARE 1915-48: THE EVOLUTION OF AN AFRICAN COLLEGE.
London, C. Hurst and Co., 1968.
New York, Humanities Press, 1968.

Afr	39	4	1969	441-2	P. H. Canham

Kilby, Peter

296   Kilby, Peter
       INDUSTRIALIZATION IN AN OPEN ECONOMY: NIGERIA, 1945-1966.
       London, Cambridge University Press, 1969.

       Af HS   3   2   1970   447-9   E. Wayne Nafziger
       JMAS   9   1   1971   150-3   A. F. Ewing

297   Kilson, Martin
       POLITICAL CHANGE IN A WEST AFRICAN STATE; A STUDY OF THE
       MODERNIZATION PROCESS IN SIERRA LEONE.
       Cambridge, Harvard University Press, 1966.

       Afr   37   4   1967   488-9   Michael Banton
       Af Af   66   265   1967   361-3   H. Millar-Craig
       Af St   27   4   1968   217-9   Noam J. Pines
       JAH   8   3   1967   565-7   Christopher Fyfe
       JMAS   6   3   1968   442-4   John S. Saul
       Race   9   1   1967/68   109-10   C. E. Welch

298   Kimambo, Isaria N.
       A POLITICAL HISTORY OF THE PARE OF TANZANIA, c.1500-1900.
       Nairobi, East African Publishing House, 1969.

       Af SR   --   12   1971   151   Ian Henderson

299   Kimble, David
       A POLITICAL HISTORY OF GHANA; THE RISE OF GOLD COAST NATIONAL-
       ISM, 1850-1928.
       Oxford, Clarendon Press, 1963.

       AHR   69   2   1963/64   462-3   Henry S. Wilson
       BSOAS   27   2   1964   490   D. H. Jones
       EHR   80   315   1965   367-9   George Shepperson
       Hist   49   166   1964   272-3   Christopher Fyfe
       JAH   5   1   1964   127-32   Adu Boahen
       JMAS   2   2   1964   324-7   David E. Apter

300   Kirk-Greene, Anthony Hamilton Millard
       ADAMAWA PAST AND PRESENT: AN HISTORICAL APPROACH TO THE DE-
       VELOPMENT OF A NORTHERN CAMEROONS PROVINCE.
       London, printed for the International African Institute by
       Oxford University Press, 1958; Reprinted by Dawsons, 1969.

       Afr   29   3   1959   316-7   E. E. Rich
       Af Af   57   229   1958   326-8   P. H. G. Scott

Kopytoff, Jean Herskovits

(Kirk-Greene, Anthony Hamilton Millard)

Af St	25	1	1966	54-5	M. D. W. Jeffreys
AHR	64	2	1958/59	435-6	Vernon McKay
BSOAS	22	2	1959	398-400	D. W. Arnott
JAH	1	1	1960	186-7	C. W. Newbury

301   Kiwanuka, M. S. M. Semakula
A HISTORY OF BUGANDA: FROM THE FOUNDATION OF THE KINGDOM TO 1900.
London, Longman, 1971.
New York, Africana Publishing Corp., 1972.

Af Af	72	286	1973	89	Christopher Wrigley
Af StR	16	3	1973	444-6	James A. Casada
Hist	59	196	1974	311	A. D. Roberts

302   Ki-Zerbo, Joseph
HISTOIRE DE L'AFRIQUE NOIRE, D'HIER À DEMAIN.
Paris, Hatier, 1972.

JAH	15	1	1974	149-50	A. D. Roberts

303   Klein, Martin A.
ISLAM AND IMPERIALISM IN SENEGAL: SINE-SALOUM, 1847-1914.
Edinburgh, Edinburgh U.P., 1968.
Stanford, Calif., published for the Hoover Institution on War, Revolution, and Peace by Stanford University Press, 1968.

AHR	74	3	1968/69	1055-6	Donald L. Wiedner
Hist	54	182	1969	464-5	Humphrey J. Fisher
JAH	10	2	1969	325-6	D. B. Cruise O'Brien

304   Klein, Martin A., comp.
PERSPECTIVES ON THE AFRICAN PAST, EDITED BY MARTIN A. KLEIN AND G. WESLEY JOHNSON.
Boston, Little, Brown, 1972.

JMAS	10	4	1972	643-5	Erving E. Beauregard

305   Kopytoff, Jean Herskovits
A PREFACE TO MODERN NIGERIA; THE "SIERRA LEONIANS" IN YORUBA, 1830-1890.
Madison, University of Wisconsin Press, 1965.

Kritzeck, James

    (Kopytoff, Jean Herskovits)
Afr	36	4	1966	452	J. B. Webster
AHR	72	3	1966/67	1047-8	L. Gray Cowan
JAH	7	3	1966	522-4	A. E. Afigbo
JMAS	4	2	1966	251-2	Robert L. Tignor

306   Kritzeck, James
ISLAM IN AFRICA, EDITED BY JAMES KRITZECK AND WILLIAM H. LEWIS.
CONTRIBUTORS: J. SPENCER TRIMINGHAM AND OTHERS.
New York, Van Nostrand-Reinhold Co., 1969.

AHR	75	7	1969/70	2101-2	Martin A. Klein
JAH	11	4	1970	609-11	J. O. Hunwick

307   Kup, A. P.
A HISTORY OF SIERRA LEONE, 1400-1787.
Cambridge, University Press, 1961.

Af Af	60	240	1961	456	G. Beresford-Stooke
Af St	27	3	1968	149-51	M. D. W. Jeffreys
BSOAS	24	3	1961	610	D. H. Jones
EHR	77	305	1962	786-7	J. D. Hargreaves
JAH	2	2	1961	327-8	Christopher Fyfe

308   Kuper, Hilda
AFRICAN LAW: ADAPTATION AND DEVELOPMENT, EDITED BY HILDA
KUPER AND LEO KUPER.
Berkeley, University of California Press, 1965.

Af Af	66	263	1967	173	-----
BSOAS	30	3	1967	746-7	James S. Read
JAH	7	3	1966	534-5	H. F. Morris
JMAS	5	1	1967	158-60	Ralph E. S. Tanner

309   Kuper, Leo
AN AFRICAN BOURGEOISIE; RACE, CLASS, AND POLITICS IN SOUTH
AFRICA.
New Haven, Yale University Press, 1965.

Af Af	64	257	1965	300-1	G. V. Doxey
JMAS	4	1	1966	115-8	L. Bloom
Race	7	2	1965/66	205-7	Michael Banton

Leakey, Louis Seymour Bazett

310   Lagergren, David
       MISSION AND STATE IN THE CONGO. A STUDY OF THE RELATIONS BE-
       TWEEN PROTESTANT MISSIONS AND THE CONGO INDEPENDENT STATE
       AUTHORITIES WITH SPECIAL REFERENCE TO THE EQUATOR DISTRICT,
       1885-1903.
       Lund, Gleerup, 1970.

Afr	43	4	1973	356	F. B. Welbourn
Af HS	4	1	1971	222-4	Charles H. Stuart
JAH	12	3	1971	509-10	Ruth Slade

311   Last, Murray
       THE SOKOTO CALIPHATE.
       Harlow, Longmans, 1967.
       New York, Humanities Press, 1967.

Afr	40	1	1970	84-5	P. M. Holt
Af HS	2	1	1969	172-4	Louis Brenner
BSOAS	34	2	1971	446-7	Mervyn Hiskett
JAH	10	3	1969	490-3	John Ralph Willis

312   Latham, A. J. H.
       OLD CALABAR, 1600-1891; THE IMPACT OF THE INTERNATIONAL ECONOMY
       UPON A TRADITIONAL SOCIETY.
       Oxford, Clarendon Press, 1973.

Af Af	73	293	1974	492-3	G. I. Jones
BSOAS	37	2	1974	514-5	Richard Gray
EHR	90	354	1975	191	Roger Anstey
Hist	59	196	1974	305	P. E. H. Hair
JAH	15	2	1974	328-30	G. I. Jones

313   Lawrence, Arnold Walter
       TRADE CASTLES AND FORTS OF WEST AFRICA.
       London, J. Cape, 1963.
       Stanford, Stanford University Press, 1964 (c1963).

Afr	36	4	1966	460	Ivor Wilks
AHR	70	4	1964/65	1215	Erving E. Beauregard
EHR	81	319	1966	392-3	J. R. Hale
JAH	5	2	1964	322-3	R. Mauny

314   Leakey, Louis Seymour Bazett
       MAU MAU AND THE KIKUYU.

Lemarchand, René

    (Leakey, Louis Seymour Bazett)
    London, Methuen, 1952.
    New York, Day, 1954.

    Afr   23 3   1953   262-3   John Middleton

315   Lemarchand, René
    POLITICAL AWAKENING IN THE BELGIAN CONGO.
    Berkeley, University of California Press, 1964.

    POLITICAL AWAKENING IN THE CONGO: THE POLITICS OF FRAGMENTA-
    TION.
    Los Angeles, University of California Press, 1965.

    Afr   38 1   1968   87   J. S. LaFontaine
    Af Af 65 259 1966   177-8   Tom Stacey
    AHR   70 4   1964/65 1214   Robert O. Collins
    JMAS   4 1   1966   111-5   Colin Legum

316   Lemarchand, René
    RWANDA AND BURUNDI.
    London, Pall Mall Press, 1970.
    New York, Praeger Publishers, 1970.

    Afr   41 2   1971   167-9   Lucy Mair
    Af Af 70 279 1971   190-1   Randall Baker
    AHR   76 3   1971   815-6   Robert I. Rotberg
    IJAHS 5 2   1972   276-8   Edouard Bustin

317   Le May, Godfrey Hugh Lancelot
    BRITISH SUPREMACY IN SOUTH AFRICA, 1899-1907.
    Oxford, Clarendon Press, 1965.

    Af Af 67 268 1968   274-5   D. M. van der H. Schreuder
    AHR   71 4   1965/66 1403-4   Richard H. Wilde
    BSOAS 29 1   1966   188-9   Anthony Atmore
    HJ   9 1   1966   149-51   Ronald Hyam
    Hist   51 173 1966   389-90   Freda Harcourt
    JAH   7 3   1966   528-30   Eric Stokes

318   Leubuscher, Charlotte
    TANGANYIKA TERRITORY, A STUDY OF ECONOMIC POLICY UNDER MANDATE.
    Issued under the auspices of the Royal Institute of Interna-
    tional Affairs, London, New York, Oxford University Press,
    1944.

Levtzion, Nehemia

(Leubuscher, Charlotte)
Afr   15   4   1945   218-20   Audrey I. Richards

319   Le Vine, Victor T.
      THE CAMEROON FEDERAL REPUBLIC.
      Ithaca, Cornell University Press, 1971.

      Af Af   72   289   1973   453-4   J. F. Bayart
      AHR   80   2   1975   450-1   Frederick Quinn
      IJAHS   6   1   1973   117-9   David E. Gardinier
      JMAS   11   2   1973   326-9   W. Norman Haupt

320   Le Vine, Victor T.
      THE CAMEROONS, FROM MANDATE TO INDEPENDENCE.
      Berkeley, University of California Press, 1964.

      Af Af   65   259   1966   181-2   C. M. Le Quesne
      BSOAS   28   3   1965   689-90   D. H. Jones
      JMAS   3   4   1965   629-30   George R. Horner
      Race   7   1   1965/66   92-3   Edwin Ardener

321   Levtzion, Nehemia
      ANCIENT GHANA AND MALI.
      London, Methuen, 1973.

      Afr   44   1   1974   103   R. Mauny
      Af Af   72   289   1973   454-5   Thomas Hodgkin
      AHR   80   2   1975   448-9   Brian M. Fagan
      Hist   59   196   1974   304   Humphrey J. Fisher
      IJAHS   8   1   1975   175-81   John Ralph Willis
      JAH   15   3   1974   479-88   P. F. de Moraes Farias

322   Levtzion, Nehemia
      MUSLIMS AND CHIEFS IN WEST AFRICA: A STUDY OF ISLAM IN THE
      MIDDLE VOLTA BASIN IN THE PRE-COLONIAL PERIOD.
      Oxford, Clarendon Press, 1968.

      Afr   40   2   1970   181-2   Phyllis Ferguson
      Af Af   68   273   1969   363-4   J. O. Hunwick
      AHR   76   2   1971   533-4   Louis Brenner
      BSOAS   32   3   1969   659-60   Mervyn Hiskett
      JAH   10   3   1969   489-90   N. Q. King

Lewis, Herbert S.

323   Lewis, Herbert S.
A GALLA MONARCHY; JIMMA ABBA JIFAR, ETHIOPIA, 1830-1932.
Madison, University of Wisconsin Press, 1965.

Afr	36	4	1966	454-5	V. Luling
Af Af	65	261	1966	363	-----
JAH	7	3	1966	516-9	M. Abir

324   Lewis, I. M.
THE MODERN HISTORY OF SOMALILAND, FROM NATION TO STATE.
New York, F. A. Praeger, 1965.

Afr	37	4	1967	491-2	P. T. W. Baxter
AHR	71	3	1965/66	1033-4	H. G. Marcus
BSOAS	29	2	1966	435-6	P. H. Gulliver
JAH	7	3	1966	530-2	E. Cerulli
JMAS	3	3	1965	445-7	Saadia Touval

325   Leys, Colin
EUROPEAN POLITICS IN SOUTHERN RHODESIA.
Oxford, Clarendon Press, 1959.

AHR	65	1	1959/60	166	Colin Rhys Lovell
JAH	1	1	1960	159-63	J. D. Fage
RLJ	--	25	1959	76-9	C. Frantz

326   Liebenow, J. Gus
COLONIAL RULE AND POLITICAL DEVELOPMENT IN TANZANIA: THE CASE
OF THE MAKONDE.
Evanston, Northwestern University Press, 1971.

Af StR	15	2	1972	322-3	Wyatt Mac Gaffey
JAH	13	2	1972	337-8	P. M. Redmond

327   Liebenow, J. Gus
LIBERIA; THE EVOLUTION OF PRIVILEGE.
Ithaca, Cornell University Press, 1969.

Af HS	3	1	1970	240-3	Jane Martin
JMAS	11	3	1973	489-92	Igolima T. D. Amachree

328   Listowel, Judith (Márffy-Mantuano) Hare, countess of
THE MAKING OF TANGANYIKA.

A Select Bibliography of Books and Reviews, 1945-1975

Lofchie, Michael F.

(Listowel, Judith (Márffy-Mantuano) Hare, countess of)
New York, London, House and Maxwell, 1965.
London, Chatto and Windus, 1965.

Af Af	66	263	1967	173	-----
JMAS	4	2	1966	270-2	John Iliffe
Race	8	1	1966/67	105-7	Robert I. Rotberg

329 Lloyd, Peter Cutt
AFRICA IN SOCIAL CHANGE.
Baltimore, Penguin Books, 1967.
Harmondsworth, Penguin, 1967.

AFRICA IN SOCIAL CHANGE; WEST AFRICAN SOCIETIES IN TRANSITION.
New York, Praeger, 1968.

Afr	38	2	1968	209-10	Pierre L. van den Berghe
Af Af	67	267	1968	160-1	Eva Krapf Askari
Af HS	1	1	1968	140-3	William O. Brown
JMAS	6	2	1968	286-90	Bernard Magubane

330 Lloyd, Peter Cutt
THE POLITICAL DEVELOPMENT OF YORUBA KINGDOMS IN THE EIGHTEENTH
AND NINETEENTH CENTURIES.
London, Royal Anthropological Institute, 1971.

| Af Af | 72 | 286 | 1973 | 76-9 | R. C. C. Law |
| JAH | 13 | 2 | 1972 | 344-5 | R. C. C. Law |

331 Lockhart, John Gilbert
CECIL RHODES; THE COLOSSUS OF SOUTHERN AFRICA, BY J. G. LOCK-
HART AND C. M. WOODHOUSE.
New York, Macmillan, 1963.

| JAH | 5 | 3 | 1964 | 457-8 | Richard Brown |
| JMAS | 2 | 2 | 1964 | 281-2 | John D. Hargreaves |

332 Lofchie, Michael F.
ZANZIBAR: BACKGROUND TO REVOLUTION.
Princeton, Princeton University Press, 1965.

Afr	38	1	1968	88-9	John Middleton
Af Af	67	266	1968	74-5	Frene N. Ginwala
AHR	72	1	1966/67	255-6	Margaret L. Bates
JMAS	6	2	1968	274-5	J. S. Rumbold

79

Louis, William Roger

333   Louis, William Roger
      GREAT BRITAIN AND GERMANY'S LOST COLONIES, 1914-1919.
      Oxford, Clarendon Press, 1967.

Af Af	67	268	1968	262-3	Hartmut Pogge von Strand- mann
AHR	73	4	1967/68	1157-8	J. S. Galbraith
IJAHS	5	3	1972	501-3	Richard Dale
JAH	9	2	1968	337-8	Roland Oliver
JAH	9	2	1968	339	Hartmut Pogge von Strand- mann

334   Louis, William Roger
      RUANDA-URUNDI, 1884-1919.
      Oxford, Clarendon Press, 1963.

Af Af	63	253	1964	307	-----
AHR	69	4	1963/64	1153	Robert O. Collins
BSOAS	27	3	1964	672-3	Jacques Maquet
EHR	80	315	1965	436-7	A. J. Hanna
Hist	49	166	1964	273	Roland Oliver
JAH	5	3	1964	464-5	Jacques Willequet

335   Low, Donald Anthony
      BUGANDA AND BRITISH OVERRULE, 1900-1955; TWO STUDIES, BY D.
      ANTHONY LOW AND R. CRANFORD PRATT.
      London, New York, published on behalf of the East African In-
      stitute of Social Research by Oxford University Press, 1960.

Afr	30	4	1960	407-9	Lucy Mair
Af Af	59	237	1960	347-8	Ernest Haddon
AHR	66	2	1960/61	512-3	Philip D. Curtin
EHR	77	302	1962	202	George Shepperson
Hist	46	156	1961	74-5	A. J. Hanna
JAH	1	2	1960	325-6	Roland Oliver
RLJ	--	31	1962	61-6	Eric Stokes

336   Low, Donald Anthony
      BUGANDA IN MODERN HISTORY.
      Berkeley, University of California Press, 1971.
      London, Weidenfeld and Nicolson, 1971.

AHR	77	5	1972	1492-3	Prosser Gifford
IJAHS	5	1	1972	106-10	John A. Rowe

337   Low, Victor N.
THREE NIGERIAN EMIRATES; A STUDY IN ORAL HISTORY.
Evanston, Northwestern University Press, 1972.

Afr	44	1	1974	96-7	Murray Last
BSOAS	37	3	1974	730-1	Humphrey J. Fisher
IJAHS	6	3	1973	509-12	Louis Brenner

338   Lusignan, Guy de
FRENCH-SPEAKING AFRICA SINCE INDEPENDENCE.
London, Pall Mall Press, 1969.
New York, Praeger, 1969.

Afr	40	2	1970	176-7	Hubert Deschamps
Af Af	69	277	1970	401-2	Martin Staniland
Af HS	3	1	1970	208-10	David E. Gardinier
Af StR	14	1	1971	142-3	Martin A. Klein
JMAS	7	4	1969	752-5	Mbella Sonne Dipoko

339   Luthuli, Albert John
LET MY PEOPLE GO; AN AUTOBIOGRAPHY.   INTROD. BY CHARLES HOOPER.
Johannesburg, Collins, 1962.
New York, McGraw-Hill, 1962.

JAH	4	1	1963	145-6	Shula Marks

340   Luwel, Marcel
SIR FRANCIS DE WINTON; ADMINISTRATEUR GÉNÉRAL DU CONGO, 1884-1886.
Tervuren, Musée royal de l'Afrique centrale, 1964.

JAH	6	3	1965	432-4	Roger Anstey

341   Lynch, Hollis Ralph
EDWARD WILMOT BLYDEN: PAN-NEGRO PATRIOT 1832-1912.
London, New York, Oxford U.P., 1967.

Af HS	1	2	1968	294-6	Christopher Fyfe
AHR	73	4	1967/68	1216	Louis Filler
BSOAS	32	1	1969	220-1	Humphrey J. Fisher
EHR	84	331	1969	431	John D. Hargreaves
JAH	9	3	1968	486-7	Robert W. July
Race	11	1	1969/70	96-7	C. W. Newbury

Lystad. Robert A.

342   Lystad, Robert A.
       THE ASHANTI; A PROUD PEOPLE.
       New Brunswick, N. J., Rutgers University Press, 1958.

       Afr   29   2   1959   211-2   M. Fortes

343   McCall, Daniel F.
       AFRICA IN TIME-PERSPECTIVE; A DISCUSSION OF HISTORICAL RECON-
       STRUCTION FROM UNWRITTEN SOURCES.
       Boston, Boston University Press, 1964.

Afr	34	4	1964	380-1	R. Mauny
Af St	29	4	1970	296-8	R. L. Cope
AHR	71	1	1965/66	267-8	D. L. Wiedner
BSOAS	28	1	1965	196-7	D. H. Jones
EHR	81	319	1966	439	Christopher Fyfe
JAH	6	1	1965	121-3	Hubert Deschamps

344   Mackenzie, William James Miller
       FIVE ELECTIONS IN AFRICA; A GROUP OF ELECTORAL STUDIES, EDITED
       BY W. J. M. MACKENZIE AND KENNETH ROBINSON.
       Oxford, Clarendon Press, 1960.

Af Af	59	235	1960	161-2	Christopher Fyfe
JAH	1	2	1960	332-5	Thomas Hodgkin

345   Mackintosh, John Pitcairn
       NIGERIAN GOVERNMENT AND POLITICS.
       London, Allen and Unwin, 1966.

       NIGERIAN GOVERNMENT AND POLITICS; PRELUDE TO THE REVOLUTION.
       Evanston, Northwestern University Press, 1966.

Af Af	66	262	1967	69-71	A. H. M. Kirk-Greene
Race	10	1	1968/69	125-6	C. E. Welch

346   Macmillan, William Miller
       THE ROAD TO SELF-RULE; A STUDY IN COLONIAL EVOLUTION.
       London, Faber and Faber, 1959.
       New York, Praeger, 1960 (c1959).

Af Af	59	237	1960	333-4	D. C. Cumming
AHR	65	4	1959/60	891-3	Paul Knaplund
JAH	1	2	1960	327-8	Philip D. Curtin

Mannoni, Dominique O.

347   Maguire, G. Andrew
      TOWARD 'UHURU' IN TANZANIA: THE POLITICS OF PARTICIPATION.
      London, Cambridge U.P., 1969.

Af Af	71	282	1972	101-3	Cherry Gertzel
Af St	30	2	1971	158-60	Nancy Charton
Hist	55	184	1970	318	Kenneth Ingham
JAH	11	4	1970	616-8	Christopher St. John
Race	12	1	1970/71	113-4	Christopher Fyfe

348   Mahood, Molly Maureen
      JOYCE CARY'S AFRICA.
      London, Methuen, 1964.
      Boston, Houghton Mifflin, 1965 (c1964).

Af Af	64	254	1965	60	Hilary Blood
JMAS	2	4	1964	615-7	Eldred Jones

349   Mainga, Mutumba
      BULOZI UNDER THE LUYANA KINGS; POLITICAL EVOLUTION AND STATE
      FORMATION IN PRE-COLONIAL ZAMBIA.
      London, Longmans, 1973.

Af Af	73	291	1974	242-3	Andrew Roberts
BSOAS	37	3	1974	726-7	John McCracken
JAH	15	3	1974	495-6	Robin Fielder

350   Mangat, J. S.
      A HISTORY OF THE ASIANS IN EAST AFRICA, c.1886 TO 1945.
      Oxford, Clarendon Press, 1969.

Af Af	71	282	1972	98-100	James S. Read
Af HS	3	1	1970	219-20	Stanley W. Liszka, Jr.
AHR	75	3	1969/70	897-8	Robert L. Tignor
BSOAS	33	1	1970	233-5	H. S. Morris
JAH	11	1	1970	160-2	Alan Smith
JMAS	7	4	1969	762-3	Sukhi Singh
Race	11	4	1969/70	522-4	Donald Denoon

351   Mannoni, Dominique O.
      PSYCHOLOGIE DE LA COLONISATION.
      Paris, Éditions du Seuil, 1950.

      PROSPERO AND CALIBAN; THE PSYCHOLOGY OF COLONIZATION. TRANS-
      LATED BY PAMELA POWESLAND. WITH A FOREWORD BY PHILIP MASON.

Mansergh, Nicholas

    (Mannoni, Dominique O.)
    New York, Praeger, 1956; 2d ed., 1964.

Afr	21	1	1951	74-5	H. Deschamps
Afr	27	3	1957	304	B. E. Wyatt
Af St	17	4	1958	224-5	S. Biesheuvel

    2d ed.

JMAS	3	4	1965	623-4	Walter Markov

352   Mansergh, Nicholas
    SOUTH AFRICA 1906-1961; THE PRICE OF MAGNANIMITY. WITH A
    FOREWORD BY WATSON KIRKCONNELL.
    London, George Allen and Unwin, Ltd., 1962.
    New York, Praeger, 1962.

Af Af	61	244	1962	258-9	Laura Longmore
AHR	68	2	1962/63	457-9	Vernon McKay

353   Maquet, Jacques Jérôme Pierre
    AFRIQUE; LES CIVILISATIONS NOIRES.
    Paris, Horizons de France, 1962.

    CIVILIZATIONS OF BLACK AFRICA. REV. AND TRANSLATED BY JOAN
    RAYFIELD.
    New York, Oxford University Press, 1972.

Afr	34	1	1964	63	G. W. B. Huntingford
BSOAS	36	3	1973	728-30	Paul Spencer
IJAHS	6	4	1973	662-5	Margaret Hay
JMAS	11	1	1973	153-4	Smart A. Ekpo

354   Maquet, Jacques Jérôme Pierre
    THE PREMISE OF INEQUALITY IN RUANDA; A STUDY OF POLITICAL
    RELATIONS IN A CENTRAL AFRICAN KINGDOM.
    London, published for the International African Institute by
    the Oxford University Press, 1961.

Afr	31	4	1961	383-6	John Beattie
Af St	22	3	1963	122-3	J. van Velsen
BSOAS	24	2	1961	392-3	G. W. B. Huntingford
JAH	3	1	1962	161-2	Jan Vansina
RLJ	--	31	1962	68-70	Ann Tweedie

355   Marais, Johannes Stephanus
       THE FALL OF KRUGER'S REPUBLIC.
       Oxford, Clarendon Press, 1961.

       Af Af   61 242 1962   57-8   Marjorie Juta
       AHR   67 2   1961/62   494   John S. Galbraith
       EHR   78 309 1963   746-8   Ethel Drus
       Hist   47 160 1962   208-9   Freda Harcourt
       JAH   3   1   1962   148-50   L. M. Thompson

356   Marcum, John A.
       THE ANGOLAN REVOLUTION.
       VOL. 1. THE ANATOMY OF AN EXPLOSION (1950-1962).
       Cambridge, M. I. T. Press, 1969- .

       AHR   75 6   1969/70   1757-8   Hollis R. Lynch
       JAH   11 2   1970   291-2   David Birmingham
       JMAS   8   1   1970   159-61   Kenneth W. Grundy

357   Marks, Shula
       RELUCTANT REBELLION: THE 1906-8 DISTURBANCES IN NATAL.
       Oxford, Clarendon Press, 1970.

       Af Af   70 281 1971   415-6   Anthony Atmore
       Af HS   4   1   1971   162-5   Martin Legassick
       Af St   31 4   1972   269-71   C. de B. Webb
       BSOAS   34 2   1971   448-9   Freda Harcourt
       HJ   16 3   1973   616-26   Ronald Hyam
       Hist   56 187 1971   312-3   Peter Hatton
       JAH   12 1   1971   155-6   Leonard Thompson

358   Marquard, Leopold
       THE PEOPLES AND POLICIES OF SOUTH AFRICA.
       London, New York, Oxford University Press, 1952.

       Af Af   52 206 1953   82-3   P. S.
       AHR   58 3   1952/53   582-3   Colin Rhys Lovell
       JMAS   1   2   1963   271-2   Julius Lewin
       Race   2   2   1960/61   87   Donald Wood

359   Marquard, Leopold
       THE STORY OF SOUTH AFRICA.
       London, Faber and Faber, 1955.

       Af Af   54 216 1955   232-3   Edwin W. Smith

Marsh, Zoë

360   Marsh, Zoë
      AN INTRODUCTION TO THE HISTORY OF EAST AFRICA, BY ZOË MARSH
      AND G. W. KINGSNORTH.
      Cambridge, University Press, 1957.

Afr	28	2	1958	173-5	Anthony Low
AHR	63	2	1957/58	457	Garland G. Parker

361   Martin, Esmond Bradley
      THE HISTORY OF MALINDI: A GEOGRAPHICAL ANALYSIS OF AN EAST
      AFRICAN COASTAL TOWN FROM THE PORTUGUESE PERIOD TO THE PRESENT.
      Nairobi, East African Literature Bureau, 1973.

Afr	44	4	1974	426	T. O. Beidelman
Af Af	74	294	1975	117-8	C. S. Nicholls
IJAHS	8	2	1975	359-60	Marguerite Ylvisaker
JAH	16	4	1975	628-9	J. E. G. Sutton

362   Martin, Phyllis
      THE EXTERNAL TRADE OF THE LOANGO COAST, 1576-1870; THE EFFECTS
      OF CHANGING COMMERCIAL RELATIONS ON THE VILI KINGDOM OF LOANGO.
      Oxford, Clarendon Press, 1972.

Af Af	74	294	1975	104-5	K. David Patterson
AHR	80	1	1975	154	Dorothy O. Helly
BSOAS	37	1	1974	270-2	P. E. H. Hair
Hist	59	196	1974	304	A. J. H. Latham
IJAHS	6	4	1973	682-5	Susan Herlin Broadhead
JAH	14	3	1973	516-7	J. Vansina

363   Mason, Philip
      THE BIRTH OF A DILEMMA; THE CONQUEST AND SETTLEMENT OF
      RHODESIA.
      Issued under the auspices of the Institute of Race Relations,
      London, New York, Oxford University Press, 1958.

Afr	29	4	1959	432-4	Max Gluckman
Af Af	58	231	1959	177-8	Mercedes Mackay
AHR	65	1	1959/60	116-7	C. W. de Kiewiet
EHR	74	293	1959	748-9	George Shepperson
Hist	44	150	1959	93-5	George Bennett
JAH	1	1	1960	159-63	J. D. Fage

364   Mason, Philip
        YEAR OF DECISION; RHODESIA AND NYASALAND IN 1960.
        London, New York, Oxford University Press, 1960.

Afr	31	4	1961	383	G. Beresford-Stooke
Af Af	60	238	1961	113-4	James Wiltshire
JAH	2	1	1961	166-8	George Shepperson
RLJ	--	30	1961	56-8	R. Robinson

365   Mathew, David, Bp.
        ETHIOPIA, THE STUDY OF A POLITY, 1540-1935.
        London, Eyre and Spottiswoode, 1947.

Afr	18	1	1948	71-2	Dennis J. Duncanson
Af Af	47	186	1948	57-8	Norman Bentwich
Hist	32	116	1947	143-5	L. S. Hollingsworth

366   Mboya, Tom
        FREEDOM AND AFTER.
        London, André Deutsch, 1963.
        Boston, Little, Brown, 1963.

JMAS	2	1	1964	137-9	H. D. Hughes

367   Meebelo, Henry S.
        REACTION TO COLONIALISM; A PRELUDE TO THE POLITICS OF INDE-
        PENDENCE IN NORTHERN ZAMBIA 1893-1939. FOREWORD BY KENNETH D.
        KAUNDA.
        Manchester, published for the Institute for African Studies,
        University of Zambia, by Manchester University Press, 1971.

Hist	57	191	1972	475	Andrew C. Ross
JAH	13	3	1972	524-5	Gerald L. Caplan
JMAS	11	2	1973	332-3	Helmuth Heisler

368   Merriam, Alan P.
        CONGO, BACKGROUND OF CONFLICT.
        Evanston, Northwestern University Press, 1961.

Afr	32	2	1962	179-81	Luc de Heusch
Af Af	61	245	1962	336-7	Czesław Jeśman
JAH	5	1	1964	145-6	Jean Stengers

Middleton, John

369   Middleton, John
      THE EFFECTS OF ECONOMIC DEVELOPMENT ON TRADITIONAL POLITICAL
      SYSTEMS IN AFRICA SOUTH OF THE SAHARA.
      The Hague, Mouton, 1966.

      JMAS   7   4   1969   749-50   Wieland W. Jaeger

370   Mlambo, Eshmael Ephial Mtshumayeli
      RHODESIA, THE STRUGGLE FOR A BIRTHRIGHT.
      London, C. Hurst, 1972.

      Af Af   73   293   1974   479-81   Anthony McAdam
      Af SR   --   17   1974   607-8   Robin Palmer
      JMAS   11   2   1973   334-5   Eno J. Usoro

371   Mokgatle, Naboth
      THE AUTOBIOGRAPHY OF AN UNKNOWN SOUTH AFRICAN.
      London, C. Hurst, 1971.
      Berkeley, University of California Press, 1971.

      Af Af   71   283   1972   216-7   Nicholas Hyman
      IJAHS   5   1   1972   170-4   Laurence Salomon
      Race   14   1   1972/73   85-6   Richard Gibson

372   Mondlane, Eduardo
      THE STRUGGLE FOR MOZAMBIQUE.
      Harmondsworth, Penguin, 1969.
      Baltimore, Penguin Books, 1969.

      Af Af   69   274   1970   81-2   David Birmingham
      JAH   10   4   1969   689-90   Roland Oliver

373   Morel, Edmund Dene
      E. D. MOREL'S HISTORY OF THE CONGO REFORM MOVEMENT; EDITED BY
      WILLIAM ROGER LOUIS AND JEAN STENGERS.
      Oxford, Clarendon Press, 1968.

      Af Af   69   277   1970   405-6   Suzanne Miers
      BSOAS   33   2   1970   436-7   David Birmingham
      Hist   54   181   1969   318   P. H. S. Hatton
      JAH   10   3   1969   507-9   Roger Anstey

Mulford, David C.

374   Morgenthau, Ruth Schachter
       POLITICAL PARTIES IN FRENCH-SPEAKING WEST AFRICA.
       Oxford, Clarendon Press, 1964.

Afr	35	2	1965	215	Lucy Mair
Af Af	64	257	1965	308-10	C. M. Le Quesne
JAH	6	2	1965	240-3	Georges Fischer
JMAS	3	2	1965	299-301	Francis X. Sutton
Race	6	4	1964/65	345-6	Claude Welch

375   Morris, Donald R.
       THE WASHING OF THE SPEARS; A HISTORY OF THE RISE OF THE ZULU
       NATION UNDER SHAKA AND ITS FALL IN THE ZULU WAR OF 1879.
       New York, Simon and Schuster, 1965.
       London, Cape, 1966.

JAH	8	3	1967	529-40	Shula Marks

376   Mortimer, Edward
       FRANCE AND THE AFRICANS, 1944-1960: A POLITICAL HISTORY.
       London, Faber, 1969.
       New York, Walker, 1969.

Afr	40	1	1970	83	Hubert Deschamps
Af Af	69	275	1970	188-9	R. W. Johnson
Hist	55	184	1970	314	A. S. Kanya-Forstner
JAH	11	2	1970	296	John D. Hargreaves
JMAS	7	4	1969	752-5	Mbella Sonne Dipoko

377   Mosley, Leonard Oswald
       HAILE SELASSIE I: THE CONQUERING LION.
       London, Weidenfeld and Nicolson, 1964.

       HAILE SELASSIE: THE CONQUERING LION.
       Englewood Cliffs, N. J., Prentice-Hall, 1965 (c1964).

JMAS	3	2	1965	314-5	Percy Arnold

378   Mulford, David C.
       THE NORTHERN RHODESIA GENERAL ELECTION, 1962.
       Nairobi, Oxford University Press, 1964.

Afr	35	2	1965	220-1	Lucy Mair

Mulford, David C.

379 Mulford, David C.
     ZAMBIA: THE POLITICS OF INDEPENDENCE, 1957-1964.
     London, Oxford U.P., 1967.

     Af Af 67 267 1968   174-5   Christopher R. Hill
     JAH   9   3 1968   494-6   Mutumba Bull
     Race   9   4 1967/68 529-31   Robert I. Rotberg

380 Muller, C. F. J.
     DIE BRITSE OWERHEID EN DIE GROOT TREK.
     Kaapstad, Juta, 1948.

     AHR   58   3   1952/53 582-3   Colin Rhys Lovell
     Hist   39 135-6 1954   160-1   A. F. H.

381 Muller, C. F. J.
     VYFHONDERD JAAR SUID-AFRIKAANSE GESKIEDENIS. ONDER REDAKSIE
     VAN C. F. J. MULLER.
     Pretoria, Academica, 1968.

     FIVE HUNDRED YEARS; A HISTORY OF SOUTH AFRICA; EDITED BY
     C. F. J. MULLER.
     Pretoria, Academica, 1969.

     Af HS   3   2   1970   491-6   Martin Legassick
     JAH   11   3   1970   435-47   Shula Marks

382 Mungeam, Gordon Hudson
     BRITISH RULE IN KENYA, 1895-1912: THE ESTABLISHMENT OF AD-
     MINISTRATION IN THE EAST AFRICA PROTECTORATE.
     Oxford, Clarendon Press, 1966.

     AHR   73   1   1967/68 194   Margaret L. Bates
     BSOAS 30   3   1967   740-1   Kenneth Ingham
     EHR   84 330   1969   207-8   George Shepperson
     Hist   53 178   1968   297-8   O. W. Furley
     JAH   8   3   1967   551-3   D. A. Low
     Race   8   4   1966/67 425-6   Lucy Mair

383 Murdock, George Peter
     AFRICA: ITS PEOPLES AND THEIR CULTURE HISTORY.
     New York, McGraw-Hill, 1959.

     Afr   30   3   1960   277-8   G. W. B. Huntingford
     Af Af 59 234 1960   72-3   H. V. L. Swanzy

```
(Murdock, George Peter)
AHR      65   4    1959/60   871-2     Philip D. Curtin
JAH       2   2    1961      299-309   J. D. Fage
```

384   Murray-Brown, Jeremy
       KENYATTA.
       London, G. Allen and Unwin, 1972.
       New York, E. P. Dutton, 1973 (c1972).

```
IJAHS    8    4    1975      699-702   Roderick J. Macdonald
JAH     14    3    1973      521-2     Frank Furedi
```

385   Musson, Margaret
       AGGREY OF ACHIMOTA, BY M. MUSSON, WITH A FOREWORD BY A. G.
       FRASER.
       London and Redhill, United Society for Christian Literature,
       1944.

```
Afr     15    3    1945      171-2     Edwin W. Smith
```

386   Mwase, George Simeon
       STRIKE A BLOW AND DIE; A NARRATIVE OF RACE RELATIONS IN
       COLONIAL AFRICA.   EDITED AND INTRODUCED BY ROBERT I. ROTBERG.
       Cambridge, Harvard University Press, 1967.

```
Afr     39    2    1969      194-5     T. Price
Af St   27    3    1968      151-2     Julius Lewin
EHR     84  333    1969      880-1     Andrew C. Ross
JAH     11    1    1970      159-60    George Shepperson
JMAS     6    2    1968      282-4     John McCracken
Race    10    2    1968/69   238       Christopher Fyfe
```

387   Nair, Kannan K.
       POLITICS AND SOCIETY IN SOUTH EASTERN NIGERIA, 1841-1906; A
       STUDY OF POWER, DIPLOMACY AND COMMERCE IN OLD CALABAR.
       London, F. Cass, 1972.

```
Af Af   73  293    1974      492-3     G. I. Jones
AHR     80    4    1975      1020      Jean Herskovits
BSOAS   36    3    1973      721-2     A. J. H. Latham
Hist    59  196    1974      306       Christopher Fyfe
JAH     14    2    1973      343-5     G. I. Jones
```

Neumark, Solomon Daniel

388   Neumark, Solomon Daniel
       FOREIGN TRADE AND ECONOMIC DEVELOPMENT IN AFRICA: A HISTORI-
       CAL PERSPECTIVE.
       Stanford, Food Research Institute, Stanford University, 1964.

       AHR   70   2   1964/65   552   George E. Brooks
       JAH   6   2   1965   245-7   Cyril Ehrlich
       JMAS   3   3   1965   454-6   A. F. Ewing

389   Newbury, Colin W.
       THE WESTERN SLAVE COAST AND ITS RULERS: EUROPEAN TRADE AND
       ADMINISTRATION AMONG THE YORUBA AND ADJA-SPEAKING PEOPLES OF
       SOUTH-WESTERN NIGERIA, SOUTHERN DAHOMEY AND TOGO.
       Oxford, Clarendon Press, 1961.

       Afr   32   4   1962   403   P. C. Lloyd
       Af Af   61 245   1962   350-1   -----
       AHR   68   2   1962/63   535-6   Vernon McKay
       BSOAS   25   3   1962   644-5   D. H. Jones
       EHR   78 309   1963   805-6   J. D. Hargreaves
       Hist   48 163   1963   252-3   Kenneth Robinson
       JAH   3   3   1962   519-21   I. A. Akinjogbin

390   Newitt, M. D. D.
       PORTUGUESE SETTLEMENT ON THE ZAMBESI; EXPLORATION, LAND TENURE,
       AND COLONIAL RULE IN EAST AFRICA.
       London, Longman, 1973.
       New York, Africana Pub. Co., 1973.

       Af Af   73 292   1974   372-4   David Birmingham
       BSOAS   38   1   1975   204-5   Richard Gray
       JAH   15   2   1974   336-8   Gerhard Liesegang

391   Niane, Djibril Tamsir
       HISTOIRE DE L'AFRIQUE OCCIDENTALE, PAR DJIBRIL TAMSIR NIANE
       ET J. SURET-CANALE.
       Paris, Présence Africaine, 1961.

       JAH   4   1   1963   153-4   Godfrey N. Brown

392   Nicholls, Christine Stephanie
       THE SWAHILI COAST: POLITICS, DIPLOMACY AND TRADE ON THE EAST
       AFRICAN LITTORAL, 1798-1856.
       London, Allen and Unwin, 1971.
       New York, Africana Pub. Corp., 1971.

Nkrumah, Kwame

(Nicholls, Christine Stephanie)

Af StR	16	2	1973	296-8	Walter T. Brown
BSOAS	35	2	1972	418-9	W. H. Whiteley
EHR	89	350	1974	203-4	Humphrey J. Fisher
Hist	58	193	1973	324	John Lonsdale
IJAHS	5	2	1972	318-9	Norman R. Bennett
JAH	15	1	1974	170-1	Roderick J. MacDonald

393 Nicolson, I. F.
THE ADMINISTRATION OF NIGERIA, 1900-1960: MEN, METHODS AND
MYTHS.
Oxford, Clarendon Press, 1969.

Afr	40	3	1970	289	Lucy Mair
EHR	87	343	1972	446-7	P. E. H. Hair
Hist	56	187	1971	313	Christopher Fyfe
JMAS	9	1	1971	153-6	J. A. Ballard

394 NIGERIAN POLITICS AND MILITARY RULE: PRELUDE TO THE CIVIL
WAR; EDITED BY S. K. PANTER-BRICK.
London, University of London, published for the Institute of
Commonwealth Studies by the Athlone Press, 1970.

Afr	41	2	1971	167-9	Lucy Mair
Af HS	4	1	1971	211-2	Henry L. Bretton
JMAS	8	3	1970	483-5	Michael Crowder
Race	12	4	1970/71	513-4	William Gutteridge
RT	--	242	1971	319-20	-----

395 Nkrumah, Kwame
GHANA; THE AUTOBIOGRAPHY OF KWAME NKRUMAH.
New York, Edinburgh, Nelson, 1957.

Afr	27	4	1957	409-10	A. M.
Af Af	56	224	1957	238-9	T. O. Elias

396 Nkrumah, Kwame
TOWARDS COLONIAL FREEDOM; AFRICA IN THE STRUGGLE AGAINST WORLD
IMPERIALISM.
London, Heinemann, 1962.

JMAS	1	1	1963	125-6	Colin Legum

Nørregaard, Georg

397   Nørregaard, Georg
       DANISH SETTLEMENTS IN WEST AFRICA, 1658-1850. TRANSLATED BY
       SIGURD MAMMEN.
       Boston, Boston University Press, 1966.

Afr	37	3	1967	366-7	Christopher Fyfe
AHR	73	1	1967/68	191-2	Harry R. Rudin
EHR	83	328	1968	610-1	C. W. Newbury
JAH	9	1	1968	162-4	Ivor Wilks

398   Nye, Joseph S.
       PAN-AFRICANISM AND EAST AFRICAN INTEGRATION.
       Cambridge, Harvard University Press, 1965.

       PAN-AFRICANISM AND EAST AFRICAN FEDERATION.
       London, Harvard University Press, Oxford University Press,
       1965.

Afr	36	4	1966	456	George Bennett
Af Af	66	263	1967	166-7	George Bennett
JMAS	3	4	1965	633-5	Aaron Segal
Race	9	2	1967/68	256-7	Christopher R. Hill

399   Nyerere, Julius Kambarage
       FREEDOM AND UNITY: UHURU NA UMOJA; A SELECTION FROM WRITINGS
       AND SPEECHES, 1952-65.
       London, Nairobi, Oxford U.P., 1967.

Af Af	66	264	1967	266-7	Robert Chambers
JAH	9	4	1968	668-9	Michael Twaddle
JMAS	6	3	1968	407-8	Jitendra Mohan
RT	--	228	1967	455-61	Dennis Austin

400   Obichere, Boniface I.
       WEST AFRICAN STATES AND EUROPEAN EXPANSION; THE DAHOMEY-NIGER
       HINTERLAND, 1885-1898.
       New Haven, Yale University Press, 1971.

Af Af	71	285	1972	457	A. S. Kanya-Forstner
AHR	80	1	1975	152-3	L. Gray Cowan
IJAHS	5	1	1972	149-50	John D. Hargreaves
JAH	13	4	1972	695-7	David S. Henige
Race	15	2	1973/74	278-9	Robert I. Rotberg

Ọlọruntimẹhin, B. O.

401   Odinga, Ajuma Oginga
      NOT YET UHURU: THE AUTOBIOGRAPHY OF OGINGA ODINGA; WITH A
      FOREWORD BY KWAME NKRUMAH.
      London, Heinemann, 1967.

      JMAS   6   3   1968   407-8   Jitendra Mohan

402   Okello, John
      REVOLUTION IN ZANZIBAR.
      Nairobi, East African Pub. House, 1967.

      JMAS   6   2   1968   274-5   J. S. Rumbold

403   Oliver, Roland Anthony
      THE MISSIONARY FACTOR IN EAST AFRICA.
      London, New York, Longmans, Green, 1952.

      Afr   25   1   1955   108-9   Lyndon Harries
      Af Af   52   207   1953   163-5   Edwin W. Smith

404   Oliver, Roland Anthony
      A SHORT HISTORY OF AFRICA, BY ROLAND OLIVER AND J. D. FAGE.
      Baltimore, Penguin Books, 1962.
      New York, New York University Press, 1963.

      Afr   33   2   1963   157   George Shepperson
      Af Af   61   245   1962   352   -----
      AHR   68   2   1962/63   453-4   Robert O. Collins
      Race   4   1   1962/63   123-4   Basil Davidson

405   Oliver, Roland Anthony
      SIR HARRY JOHNSTON AND THE SCRAMBLE FOR AFRICA.
      London, Chatto and Windus, 1957.
      New York, St. Martin's Press, 1958 (c1957).

      Afr   28   4   1958   377-9   Anthony Low
      Af Af   57   226   1958   76-7   S. S.
      BSOAS   21   2   1958   432-4   H. Moyse-Bartlett
      EHR   73   287   1958   319-21   George Shepperson
      Hist   43   148   1958   163-4   J. D. Hargreaves

406   Ọlọruntimẹhin, B. O.
      THE SEGU TUKULOR EMPIRE.
      London, Longman, 1972.

Olusanya, Gabriel Olakunle

(Oloruntimehin, B. O.)

Af Af	72	286	1973	84	Michael Brett
BSOAS	36	1	1973	196-7	Humphrey J. Fisher
Hist	60	199	1975	248-9	D. H. Jones
IJAHS	6	4	1973	646-56	David Robinson
JAH	14	3	1973	511-2	A. S. Kanya-Forstner

407   Olusanya, Gabriel Olakunle
THE SECOND WORLD WAR AND POLITICS IN NIGERIA, 1939-1953.
London, Evans Bros. for University of Lagos, 1973.

Af Af	73	290	1974	111-2	Jonathan Derrick
JAH	15	2	1974	334-6	A. H. M. Kirk-Greene
JMAS	12	3	1974	498-500	Daniel A. Offiong

408   Omari, T. Peter
KWAME NKRUMAH: THE ANATOMY OF AN AFRICAN DICTATORSHIP, BY
T. PETER OMARI; WITH A FOREWORD BY NII AMAA OLLENNU.
London, C. Hurst and Co., 1970.
New York, Africana Pub. Corp., 1970.

Afr	42	1	1972	71-2	A. H. M. Kirk-Greene
AHR	77	3	1972	814-5	Van Mitchell Smith
IJAHS	5	4	1973	661-4	Henry L. Bretton
JMAS	9	4	1971	657-60	Jitendra Mohan

409   Omer-Cooper, John D.
THE ZULU AFTERMATH; A NINETEENTH-CENTURY REVOLUTION IN BANTU
AFRICA.
London, Longmans, 1966.
Evanston, Northwestern University Press, 1966.

Afr	37	3	1967	358-9	W. D. Hammond-Tooke
AHR	72	2	1966/67	661-2	Robert O. Collins
JAH	8	3	1967	529-40	Shula Marks

410   Osogo, John
A HISTORY OF THE BALUYIA.
Nairobi, New York, Oxford University Press, 1966.

| JAH | 9 | 1 | 1968 | 177-8 | Gideon S. Were |

Pankhurst, Richard Keir Pethick

411   Owusu, Maxwell
USES AND ABUSES OF POLITICAL POWER; A CASE STUDY OF CONTINUITY
AND CHANGE IN THE POLITICS OF GHANA.
Chicago, University of Chicago Press, 1970.

Af Af	72	287	1973	204-6	Alan Cawson
JMAS	9	4	1971	657-60	Jitendra Mohan

412   Pachai, Bridglal
THE INTERNATIONAL ASPECTS OF THE SOUTH AFRICAN INDIAN QUESTION,
1860-1971.
Cape Town, C. Struik, 1971.

IJAHS	6	1	1973	141-6	Maynard W. Swanson
JAH	14	3	1973	523-7	Hugh Tinker
JMAS	13	1	1975	172-3	T. G. Ramamurthi

413   Pachai, Bridglal
MALAWI; THE HISTORY OF THE NATION.
London, Longman, 1973.

Afr	44	3	1974	320	Lucy Mair
Af Af	73	293	1974	475	George Shepperson
Hist	60	199	1975	253-4	Douglas L. Wheeler
JAH	15	2	1974	338-9	John McCracken

414   Panikkar, Kavalam Madhusudan
THE SERPENT AND THE CRESCENT; A HISTORY OF THE NEGRO EMPIRES
OF WESTERN AFRICA.
London, New York, Asia Pub. House, 1963, 1964.

Afr	35	1	1965	108-9	R. M.
BSOAS	28	1	1965	199-200	H. J. Fisher

415   Pankhurst, Estelle Sylvia
ETHIOPIA, A CULTURAL HISTORY. WITH A FOREWORD BY CANON JOHN A.
DOUGLAS.
Essex, Eng., Lalibela House, 1955.

Afr	26	4	1956	414	Edward Ullendorff

416   Pankhurst, Richard Keir Pethick
ECONOMIC HISTORY OF ETHIOPIA, 1800-1935.
Addis Ababa, Haile Sellassie I University Press, 1968.

Pankhurst, Richard Keir Pethick

      (Pankhurst, Richard Keir Pethick)

Af HS	4	2	1971	401-2	Robert L. Hess
JAH	12	3	1971	503-4	Peter Garreston
JMAS	9	3	1971	490-2	Richard A. Caulk

417   Pankhurst, Richard Keir Pethick
      AN INTRODUCTION TO THE ECONOMIC HISTORY OF ETHIOPIA, FROM
      EARLY TIMES TO 1800.
      London, Lalibela House; distributed by Sidgwick and Jackson,
      1961.

Af Af	61	243	1962	167-8	-----
AHR	67	4	1961/62	1113	Donald N. Levine
Hist	47	161	1962	345	Roland Oliver
JAH	3	1	1962	147-8	C. F. Beckingham

418   Paton, Alan
      HOFMEYR.
      London, Oxford University Press, 1964.

Af Af	64	255	1965	120-1	Hilary Blood
Af St	33	1	1974	69-71	Julius Lewin
Hist	50	170	1965	401-2	J. L. McCracken
JAH	6	3	1965	434-6	Shula Marks
Race	6	4	1964/65	269-80	Jonty Driver

419   Patterson, Sheila
      COLOUR AND CULTURE IN SOUTH AFRICA; A STUDY OF THE STATUS OF
      THE CAPE COLOURED PEOPLE WITHIN THE SOCIAL STRUCTURE OF THE
      UNION OF SOUTH AFRICA.
      London, Routledge and Paul, 1953.

Af St	12	3	1953	137-8	Julius Lewin

420   Patterson, Sheila
      THE LAST TREK; A STUDY OF THE BOER PEOPLE AND THE AFRIKANER
      NATION.
      London, Routledge and Paul, 1957.

Af Af	56	224	1957	241-2	A. C. Jacobs

421   Perham, Margery Freda
      THE COLONIAL RECKONING.
      London, Collins, 1961.

Perham, Margery Freda

(Perham, Margery Freda)
THE COLONIAL RECKONING; THE END OF IMPERIAL RULE IN AFRICA IN
THE LIGHT OF BRITISH EXPERIENCE.
New York, Knopf, 1962.

Afr	32	4	1962	400-1	Gwendolen M. Carter
AHR	68	2	1962/63	457-9	Vernon McKay

422   Perham, Margery Freda
COLONIAL SEQUENCE, 1949 TO 1969: A CHRONOLOGICAL COMMENTARY
UPON BRITISH COLONIAL POLICY IN AFRICA.
London, Methuen, 1970.

Af St	31	1	1972	51-4	T. R. H. Davenport
JMAS	9	4	1971	647-9	P. B. Harris

423   Perham, Margery Freda
THE GOVERNMENT OF ETHIOPIA.
London, Faber and Faber, 1948, 1969.
New York, Oxford University Press, 1948.
Evanston, Northwestern University Press, 1969.

Afr	18	4	1948	309-10	S. F. Nadel
Af Af	68	273	1969	372-3	N. E. Mustoe
BSOAS	32	3	1969	665-6	A. K. Irvine
JMAS	9	3	1971	498-505	James C. N. Paul

424   Perham, Margery Freda
LUGARD.
VOL. 1.   THE YEARS OF ADVENTURE, 1858-1898.
VOL. 2.   THE YEARS OF AUTHORITY, 1898-1945.
London, Collins, 1956-60.

Vol. 1

Afr	27	3	1957	289-90	L. P. Mair
Af Af	56	222	1957	81-2	C. R. S. Pitman
AHR	63	1	1957/58	183-4	Colin Rhys Lovell
EHR	73	286	1958	116-20	George Shepperson
HJC	13	2	1957	198-200	J. D. Hargreaves
JMAS	2	2	1964	283-4	John D. Hargreaves

Vol. 2

Afr	31	2	1961	185-6	Hailey
Af Af	60	240	1961	460-2	Hilary Blood
AHR	66	4	1960/61	1098-9	Philip D. Curtin

Peterson, John

(Perham, Margery Freda)					
JAH	2	2	1961	332-7	Kenneth Robinson
JMAS	2	2	1964	283-4	John D. Hargreaves

425   Peterson, John
PROVINCE OF FREEDOM; A HISTORY OF SIERRA LEONE, 1787-1870.
Evanston, Northwestern University Press, 1969.
London, Faber, 1969.

Af St	31	1	1972	39	C. C. Saunders
AHR	76	2	1971	536-7	J. F. Ade Ajayi
BSOAS	34	2	1971	445-6	Humphrey J. Fisher
Hist	56	187	1971	310-1	John Davidson
JAH	11	2	1970	284-5	John D. Hargreaves

426   Phillips, John Frederick Vicars
KWAME NKRUMAH AND THE FUTURE OF AFRICA.
London, Faber and Faber, 1960.
New York, Praeger, 1961 (c1960).

JAH	2	2	1961	342-6	Colin Legum

427   Pienaar, S.
SOUTH AFRICA; TWO VIEWS OF SEPARATE DEVELOPMENT: SAFEGUARDING
THE NATIONS OF SOUTH AFRICA, BY S. PIENAAR. OLD FALLACIES
WITH A NEW LOOK; IGNORING THE AFRICANS, BY ANTHONY SAMPSON.
London, New York, Oxford University Press, 1960.

Afr	31	1	1961	89	Sheila Patterson
Af Af	59	237	1960	340-1	Doris V. Thompson
JAH	1	2	1960	329-32	J. D. Fage
Race	2	1	1960	71-2	Charles Janson

428   Pike, John G.
MALAWI: A POLITICAL AND ECONOMIC HISTORY.
London, Pall Mall Press, 1968, 1969.
New York, F. A. Praeger, 1968.

AHR	75	3	1969/70	898-9	Marcia Wright
JAH	11	1	1970	163	George Shepperson
JMAS	7	3	1969	546-7	John McCracken
Race	10	2	1968	235-7	Robert I. Rotberg

Porter, Arthur T.

429   Pinto, Françoise Latour da Veiga
       LE PORTUGAL ET LE CONGO AU XIXe SIÈCLE; ÉTUDE D'HISTOIRE DES
       RELATIONS INTERNATIONALES. PRÉF. DE JACQUES FREYMOND. 1. ÉD.
       Paris, Presses Universitaires de France, 1972.

       JAH   15 1   1974   158-60   Roger Anstey

430   Plaatje, Solomon Tshekisho
       THE BOER WAR DIARY OF SOL T. PLAATJE; AN AFRICAN AT MAFEKING.
       EDITED BY JOHN L. COMAROFF.
       Johannesburg, Macmillan, 1973.

       Af SR   -- 17   1974   599-601   Q. N. Parsons
       JAH   15 2   1974   341-3   P. L. Bonner

431   POLITICS AND CHANGE IN DEVELOPING COUNTRIES: STUDIES IN THE
       THEORY AND PRACTICE OF DEVELOPMENT; EDITED BY COLIN LEYS FOR
       THE INSTITUTE OF DEVELOPMENT STUDIES AT THE UNIVERSITY OF
       SUSSEX.
       London, Cambridge U.P., 1969.

       Afr   40 2   1970   194   -----
       Af St   30 2   1971   160-1   Noam J. Pines
       Af StR 14 1   1971   156-7   Christian P. Potholm
       JMAS   9 3   1971   474-6   Samuel Humes
       Race   12 2   1970/71   262-3   Malcolm Cross

432   Pollock, Norman Hall
       NYASALAND AND NORTHERN RHODESIA: CORRIDOR TO THE NORTH.
       Pittsburgh, Duquesne University Press, 1971.

       AHR   80 1   1975   155-6   Franklin Parker
       JAH   15 3   1974   523   A. D. Roberts
       JMAS   11 2   1973   332-3   Helmuth Heisler

433   Porter, Arthur T.
       CREOLEDOM; A STUDY OF THE DEVELOPMENT OF FREETOWN SOCIETY.
       London, Oxford University Press, 1963; reprinted with correc-
       tions, 1966.

       Af Af   63 250 1964   79-80   Kenneth Little
       Af St   27 4   1968   217-9   Noam J. Pines
       AHR   69 3   1963/64   846-7   Philip D. Curtin
       BSOAS   27 1   1964   237-8   D. H. Jones

Post, Kenneth William John

    (Porter, Arthur T.)
JAH	4	3	1963	468-9	J. D. Hargreaves
Race	5	1	1963/64	97-8	Christopher Fyfe

434   Post, Kenneth William John
THE NIGERIAN FEDERAL ELECTION OF 1959; POLITICS AND ADMINIS-
TRATION IN A DEVELOPING POLITICAL SYSTEM.
London, published for the Nigerian Institute of Social and
Economic Research, Oxford University Press, 1963.

Af Af	63	250	1964	80-1	Alan Burns
JMAS	2	1	1964	128-30	Charles R. Nixon

435   Post, Kenneth William John
THE PRICE OF LIBERTY; PERSONALITY AND POLITICS IN COLONIAL
NIGERIA, BY KENNETH W. J. POST AND GEORGE D. JENKINS.
Cambridge, University Press, 1973.

Af Af	73	293	1974	493-6	Gavin Williams
AHR	78	5	1973	1507-8	L. Gray Cowan
Hist	59	196	1974	307-8	D. H. Jones
JAH	14	3	1973	514-6	David Craig Dorward
JMAS	12	1	1974	144-5	Bernard Nkemdirim

436   Post, Kenneth William John
STRUCTURE AND CONFLICT IN NIGERIA, 1960-1966, BY KENNETH POST
AND MICHAEL VICKERS.
London, Heinemann Educational, 1973.
Madison, University of Wisconsin Press, 1973.

Af Af	73	290	1974	114-5	Gavin Williams
IJAHS	8	1	1975	170-2	Donald Rothchild
JAH	16	1	1975	150-2	Robin Cohen
JMAS	12	2	1974	336-8	S. Egite Oyovbaire

437   Priestley, Margaret
WEST AFRICAN TRADE AND COAST SOCIETY; A FAMILY STUDY.
London, Oxford University Press, 1969.

Afr	40	4	1970	397-8	J. Ayodele Langley
Af Af	69	275	1970	189-90	Christopher Fyfe
Af HS	3	2	1970	470-4	H. M. Feinberg
AHR	75	5	1969/70	1500-1	Hollis R. Lynch
BSOAS	35	1	1972	210-1	D. H. Jones

Ranger, Terence O.

(Priestley, Margaret)
```
Hist    55  183  1970      153-4     Christopher Fyfe
JAH     11  3    1970      455-6     J. D. Fage
```

438   Pyrah, G. B.
IMPERIAL POLICY AND SOUTH AFRICA, 1902-10.
Oxford, Clarendon Press, 1955.

```
AHR     61  1    1955/56   175-6     Paul Knaplund
EHR     71  279  1956      346-7     C. H. D. Howard
Hist    42  145  1957      157-8     Alan F. Hattersley
```

439   Randles, W. G. L.
L'ANCIEN ROYAUME DU CONGO DES ORIGINES À LA FIN DU XIXe SIÈCLE.
Paris, La Haye, Mouton, 1968.

```
Afr     40  3    1970      279       Phyllis Martin
Af HS   3   1    1970      202-4     Jan Vansina
BSOAS   33  3    1970      684-5     Richard Gray
JAH     11  3    1970      450-2     David Birmingham
```

440   Ranger, Terence O.
THE AFRICAN VOICE IN SOUTHERN RHODESIA, 1898-1930.
Evanston, Northwestern University Press, 1970.
London, Heinemann Educational, 1970.
Nairobi, East African Publishing House, 1970.

```
JMAS    9   2    1971      321-4     Donald Denoon
```

441   Ranger, Terence O.
REVOLT IN SOUTHERN RHODESIA, 1896-7: A STUDY IN AFRICAN
RESISTANCE.
London, Heinemann, 1967.
Evanston, Northwestern University Press, 1967.

```
Afr     41  2    1971      174-5     Richard P. Werbner
Af Af   69  276  1970      304-5     John Lonsdale
Af HS   1   1    1968      105-7     Robert I. Rotberg
Af SR   --  7    1969      570       Ian Henderson
AHR     73  5    1967/68   1593      Leslie Clement Duly
Hist    54  180  1969      150       A. J. Hanna
JAH     9   3    1968      489-91    Roland Oliver
JMAS    7   1    1969      170-2     Richard Brown
Race    9   4    1967/68   529-31    Robert I. Rotberg
```

Redkey, Edwin S.

442   Redkey, Edwin S.
      BLACK EXODUS; BLACK NATIONALIST AND BACK-TO-AFRICA MOVEMENTS,
      1890-1910.
      New Haven, Yale University Press, 1969.

Af Af	70	278	1971	85-6	Q. N. Parsons
IJAHS	5	1	1972	129-31	Wolfe W. Schmokel
JAH	12	1	1971	167-8	George Shepperson

443   Renault, François
      LAVIGERIE, L'ESCLAVAGE AFRICAIN, ET L'EUROPE, 1868-1892.
      Paris, E. de Boccard, 1971.

Afr	42	1	1972	68-9	Hubert Deschamps
AHR	80	2	1975	449-50	J. R. Hooker
IJAHS	6	3	1973	503-4	Norman R. Bennett
JAH	14	1	1973	147-9	Suzanne Miers

444   Richards, Audrey Isabel
      EAST AFRICAN CHIEFS; A STUDY OF POLITICAL DEVELOPMENT IN SOME
      UGANDA AND TANGANYIKA TRIBES.
      London, published for the East African Institute of Social
      Research by Faber and Faber, 1960.
      New York, Praeger, 1960 (c1959).

Afr	31	1	1961	86-7	W. H. Whiteley
Af Af	59	237	1960	350-1	Ernest Haddon

445   Ritter, E. A.
      SHAKA ZULU; THE RISE OF THE ZULU EMPIRE.
      London, New York, Longmans, Green, 1955.
      New York, Putnam, 1957 (c1955).

Af Af	54	217	1955	318-9	J. P.

446   Roberts, Andrew
      A HISTORY OF THE BEMBA; POLITICAL GROWTH AND CHANGE IN NORTH-
      EASTERN ZAMBIA BEFORE 1900.
      Madison, University of Wisconsin Press, 1973.

Af Af	74	294	1975	109-10	Aylward Shorter
Af SR	--	20	1975	831-4	Brian Garvey
Hist	60	199	1975	254-5	M. Newitt
IJAHS	8	1	1975	172-5	Harry W. Langworthy
JAH	16	1	1975	145-7	Joseph C. Miller

447   Roberts, Andrew
TANZANIA BEFORE 1900. ANDREW ROBERTS, EDITOR. CONTRIBUTORS:
BEVERLY BROCK AND OTHERS.
Nairobi, published for the Historical Association of Tanzania
by the East African Pub. House, 1968.

Afr	39	4	1969	442-3	T. O. Beidelman
Af HS	3	1	1970	204-6	C. F. Holmes
Af SR	--	9	1970	705-6	Ian Henderson
BSOAS	34	1	1971	215	Anthony Atmore
JAH	10	3	1969	497-9	Roland Oliver

448   Robinson, Kenneth
THE DILEMMAS OF TRUSTEESHIP; ASPECTS OF BRITISH COLONIAL
POLICY BETWEEN THE WARS. WITH A PREFACE BY WATSON KIRKCONNELL.
London, New York, Oxford University Press, 1965.

Af Af	64	256	1965	229	Iain Gunn
JMAS	4	1	1966	119-20	Walter Markov

449   Robinson, Kenneth
ESSAYS IN IMPERIAL GOVERNMENT. PRESENTED TO MARGERY PERHAM
BY KENNETH ROBINSON AND FREDERICK MADDEN.
Oxford, B. Blackwell, 1963.

Afr	34	2	1964	177	Lucy Mair
JMAS	2	1	1964	127-8	T. O. Ranger

450   Robinson, Ronald
AFRICA AND THE VICTORIANS; THE CLIMAX OF IMPERIALISM IN THE
DARK CONTINENT, BY RONALD ROBINSON AND JOHN GALLAGHER, WITH
ALICE DENNY.
New York, St. Martin's Press, 1961.

AFRICA AND THE VICTORIANS; THE OFFICIAL MIND OF IMPERIALISM,
BY RONALD ROBINSON AND JOHN GALLAGHER, WITH ALICE DENNY.
London, Macmillan; New York, St. Martin's Press, 1965 (i.e.,
1966).

Af Af	61	242	1962	54	S. S.
EHR	78	307	1963	345-7	George Shepperson
HJ	7	1	1964	154-69	Ronald Hyam
Hist	48	163	1963	249-52	W. L. Burn
JAH	3	3	1962	469-91	Jean Stengers
JAH	3	3	1962	493-501	C. W. Newbury

Rodney, Walter

451   Rodney, Walter
A HISTORY OF THE UPPER GUINEA COAST, 1545-1800.
Oxford, Clarendon Press, 1970.

Afr	41	1	1971	73	Hubert Deschamps
Af HS	4	3	1971	669-89	Yves Person
AHR	76	3	1971	813-4	Daniel F. McCall
BSOAS	34	2	1971	443-4	P. E. H. Hair
Hist	56	187	1971	309-10	P. E. H. Hair
JAH	11	3	1970	453-5	Philip D. Curtin

452   Rosberg, Carl Gustav
THE MYTH OF "MAU MAU"; NATIONALISM IN KENYA, BY CARL G.
ROSBERG, JR. AND JOHN NOTTINGHAM.
Stanford, published for the Hoover Institution on War, Revolu-
tion, and Peace by Praeger, New York, 1966.

Afr	37	4	1967	492-3	Raymond E. Glazier, Jr.
JAH	8	3	1967	560-3	George Bennett
JMAS	4	3	1966	384-7	Raymond E. Glazier, Jr.

453   Rotberg, Robert I.
CHRISTIAN MISSIONARIES AND THE CREATION OF NORTHERN RHODESIA,
1880-1924.
Princeton, Princeton University Press, 1965.

Afr	36	2	1966	210-1	F. B. Welbourn
Af Af	65	260	1966	265	J. P. M.
Af SR	--	1	1966	91-4	Robin J. Fielder
Af St	25	2	1966	111-2	J. D. Davies
AHR	71	4	1965/66	1402-3	Colin Rhys Lovell
BSOAS	29	2	1966	436-8	Humphrey J. Fisher
EHR	82	323	1967	433-4	Owen Chadwick
Hist	52	176	1967	387-8	A. J. Hanna
JAH	8	1	1967	168-71	T. O. Ranger
Race	7	4	1965/66	421-2	Colin Leys

454   Rotberg, Robert I.
JOSEPH THOMSON AND THE EXPLORATION OF AFRICA.
New York, Oxford University Press, 1971.
London, Chatto and Windus, 1971.

Af StR	15	1	1972	160-1	Carolyn Barnes
AHR	77	3	1972	813-4	John P. Halstead
IJAHS	6	2	1973	340-2	Norman R. Bennett
JAH	13	3	1972	520-1	Caroline Oliver

Rubenson, Sven

455   Rotberg, Robert I.
A POLITICAL HISTORY OF TROPICAL AFRICA.
New York, Harcourt, Brace and World, 1965.

Af Af	69	274	1970	89	R. R.
BSOAS	31	1	1968	191-2	D. H. Jones
EHR	83	329	1968	863	Roger Anstey
Hist	55	183	1970	153	George Shepperson
JAH	8	1	1967	168-71	T. O. Ranger
JMAS	3	4	1965	624-5	John Iliffe

456   Rotberg, Robert I.
PROTEST AND POWER IN BLACK AFRICA. EDITED BY ROBERT I.
ROTBERG AND ALI A. MAZRUI.
New York, Oxford University Press, 1970.

Afr	42	2	1972	153-6	J. van Velsen
Af Af	71	283	1972	200-1	D. A. Low
Af HS	4	1	1971	141-4	Louis Brenner
AHR	77	2	1972	557-8	L. Gray Cowan
Race	13	2	1971/72	249-50	Christopher R. Hill

457   Rotberg, Robert I.
THE RISE OF NATIONALISM IN CENTRAL AFRICA; THE MAKING OF
MALAWI AND ZAMBIA, 1873-1964.
Cambridge, Harvard University Press, 1965.

Afr	36	4	1966	455-6	Andrew C. Ross
Af Af	65	261	1966	350-1	Richard Symonds
Af SR	--	1	1966	90-1	James R. Scarritt
Af St	28	1	1969	61-3	Noam J. Pines
AHR	71	4	1965/66	1399-1400	Harry R. Rudin
EHR	83	326	1968	215	George Shepperson
Hist	53	178	1968	295-6	A. J. Hanna
JAH	8	1	1967	168-71	T. O. Ranger
JMAS	5	3	1967	432-3	Otakar Hulec
Race	8	3	1966/67	297-8	Colin Leys

458   Rubenson, Sven
KING OF KINGS: TEWODROS OF ETHIOPIA.
Addis Ababa and Nairobi, published by Haile Sellassie I University in association with Oxford University Press, 1966.

Afr	39	4	1969	436-7	A. K. Irvine
JAH	8	2	1967	355-6	Donald Crummey

Ryder, Alan Frederick Charles

459   Ryder, Alan Frederick Charles
BENIN AND THE EUROPEANS, 1485-1897.
Harlow, Longmans, 1969.
New York, Humanities Press, 1969.

Afr	40	4	1970	384-5	Jan Vansina
Af Af	71	282	1972	92-3	Elizabeth Isichei
Af HS	4	2	1971	405-10	H. M. Feinberg
AHR	75	7	1969/70	2102-3	Philip D. Curtin
BSOAS	33	3	1970	684-5	Richard Gray

460   Sacks, Benjamin
SOUTH AFRICA: AN IMPERIAL DILEMMA; NON-EUROPEANS AND THE
BRITISH NATION, 1902-1914.
Albuquerque, University of New Mexico Press, 1967.

AHR	73	4	1967/68	1218-9	Richard H. Wilde
Hist	53	178	1968	298-9	Freda Harcourt
JMAS	5	4	1967	581-3	Pierre L. van den Berghe

461   Saint-Martin, Yves J.
L'EMPIRE TOUCOULEUR, 1848-1897.
Paris, Le Livre Africain, 1970.

Af HS	4	2	1971	393-4	Martin A. Klein

462   Samkange, Stanlake John Thompson
ORIGINS OF RHODESIA.
London, Heinemann, 1968.
New York, Praeger, 1969 (c1968).

Af Af	70	279	1971	193-4	S. I. Mudenge
Af HS	3	1	1970	236-7	Prosser Gifford
AHR	75	2	1969/70	558-9	Robert I. Rotberg
Hist	55	183	1970	152-3	Richard Brown
JAH	10	4	1969	683-4	Anthony Atmore
JMAS	9	2	1971	321-4	Donald Denoon

463   Savorgnan de Brazza, Pierre Paul François Camille, comte
BRAZZA EXPLORATEUR, L'OGOOUÉ, 1875-1879, PAR HENRI BRUNSCHWIG,
AVEC LE CONCOURS DE JEAN GLÉNISSON, MARIE-ANTOINETTE MÉNIER,
GILLES SAUTTER, ROGER SILLANS ... (ETC.).
Paris, La Haye, Mouton, 1966.

Shelton, Austin J.

(Savorgnan de Brazza)

Afr	37	2	1967	240-1	Colin Newbury
AHR	72	3	1966/67	1048-9	David E. Gardinier
AHR	78	4	1973	1111-2	David E. Gardinier
BSOAS	30	2	1967	477	D. H. Jones
JAH	8	2	1967	357	John E. Flint

464 Schapera, Isaac
GOVERNMENT AND POLITICS IN TRIBAL SOCIETIES.
London, Watts, 1956.
New York, Schocken Books, 1967.

Afr	27	4	1957	411	W. J. M. Mackenzie
Af Af	63	253	1964	311	-----
RLJ	--	22	1957	72-4	I. Cunnison

465 Schnapper, Bernard
LA POLITIQUE ET LE COMMERCE FRANÇAIS DANS LE GOLFE DE GUINÉE,
DE 1838 À 1871.
Paris, Mouton, 1961.

Afr	32	4	1962	404-5	C. W. Newbury
JAH	3	3	1962	524-5	C. W. Newbury

466 Seretse Khama
BOTSWANA, A DEVELOPING DEMOCRACY IN SOUTHERN AFRICA.
Uppsala, Scandinavian Institute of African Studies, 1970.

JMAS	11	1	1973	172-5	Willie Henderson

467 Shaloff, Stanley
REFORM IN LEOPOLD'S CONGO.
Richmond, Va., John Knox Press, 1970.

Af HS	4	2	1971	444	Roger Anstey
AHR	77	2	1972	561	Catherine Ann Cline
JAH	14	2	1973	351-2	Jean Stengers

468 Shelton, Austin J.
THE IGBO-IGALA BORDERLAND; RELIGION AND SOCIAL CONTROL IN
INDIGENOUS AFRICAN COLONIALISM.
Albany, N. Y., State University of New York Press, 1971.

Shepherd, Robert Henry Wishart

    (Shelton, Austin J.)

Afr	42	3	1972	250-1	G. I. Jones
IJAHS	5	1	1972	145	G. I. Jones
JMAS	11	1	1973	155-7	A. E. Afigbo

469   Shepherd, Robert Henry Wishart
    LOVEDALE AND LITERATURE FOR THE BANTU.
    Lovedale, C. P., South Africa, The Lovedale Press, 1945.

Afr	16	1	1946	63-4	Edwin W. Smith

470   Shepperson, George
    INDEPENDENT AFRICAN; JOHN CHILEMBWE AND THE ORIGINS, SETTING, AND SIGNIFICANCE OF THE NYASALAND NATIVE RISING OF 1915, BY GEORGE SHEPPERSON AND THOMAS PRICE.
    Edinburgh, University Press, 1958.

Afr	30	1	1960	88-90	Ian Cunnison
Af St	18	3	1959	153	Edward Roux
AHR	64	3	1958/59	702	Colin Rhys Lovell
EHR	75	296	1960	505-6	Margery Perham
Hist	44	150	1959	93-5	George Bennett
RLJ	--	28	1960	73-6	Max Gluckman

471   Shinnie, P. L.
    MEROE, A CIVILIZATION OF THE SUDAN.
    New York, F. A. Praeger, 1967.

BSOAS	31	3	1968	680-1	K. A. Kitchen
JAH	9	1	1968	159-60	A. J. Arkell

472   Shorter, Aylward
    CHIEFSHIP IN WESTERN TANZANIA: A POLITICAL HISTORY OF THE KIMBU.
    Oxford, Clarendon Press, 1972.

Afr	44	2	1974	207-8	R. G. Abrahams
Af Af	72	288	1973	341-2	Roy Abrahams
BSOAS	36	2	1973	511-2	Roland Oliver
IJAHS	6	2	1973	342-4	Gerald W. Hartwig
JAH	14	4	1973	701-2	Andrew Roberts

Sithole, Ndabaningi

473   Sillery, Anthony
      THE BECHUANALAND PROTECTORATE.
      Cape Town, New York, Oxford University Press, 1952.

Afr	24	1	1954	76	I. Schapera
Af Af	52	206	1953	76-7	W. M. Macmillan
Af St	12	2	1953	89	Julius Lewin

474   Sillery, Anthony
      SECHELE; THE STORY OF AN AFRICAN CHIEF.
      Oxford, G. Ronald, 1954.

Afr	25	2	1955	201-2	Edwin W. Smith
Af Af	54	214	1955	65-6	Sir Stewart Symes

475   Simons, Harold Jack
      CLASS AND COLOUR IN SOUTH AFRICA, 1850-1950, BY H. J. AND
      R. E. SIMONS.
      Harmondsworth, Penguin, 1969.

Af Af	69	275	1970	195-6	Rick Johnstone
AHR	75	6	1969/70	1758-60	Leonard Thompson
IJAHS	5	3	1972	498-500	R. Hunt Davis, Jr.
JMAS	9	4	1971	661-3	Graham C. Kinloch
Race	12	3	1970/71	379-81	Adrian Leftwich
Race	12	4	1970/71	495-500	Leo Kuper

476   Singh, Makhan
      HISTORY OF KENYA'S TRADE UNION MOVEMENT, TO 1952.
      Nairobi, East African Pub. House, 1969.

Af HS	3	2	1970	477-9	J. R. Hooker
AHR	75	6	1969/70	1756-7	Donald C. Savage
JAH	11	3	1970	465-6	Alice H. Amsden

477   Sithole, Ndabaningi
      AFRICAN NATIONALISM. WITH A FOREWORD BY R. S. GARFIELD TODD.
      Cape Town, New York, Oxford University Press, 1959.

Af Af	59	235	1960	162-4	David Dean
Af SR	--	9	1970	690-700	John Day
JAH	1	2	1960	328-9	Thomas Hodgkin
Race	2	1	1960/61	75-6	Dennis Austin
Race	10	4	1968/69	533-4	Bala Pillay

Sklar, Richard L.

478 Sklar, Richard L.
     NIGERIAN POLITICAL PARTIES; POWER IN AN EMERGENT AFRICAN
     NATION.
     Princeton, Princeton University Press, 1963.

Afr	34	4	1964	379-80	Lucy Mair
Af Af	63	253	1964	297-8	Iain Gunn
JMAS	2	1	1964	128-30	Charles R. Nixon
Race	6	3	1964/65	253-4	Claude Welch

479 Slade, Ruth M.
     ENGLISH-SPEAKING MISSIONS IN THE CONGO INDEPENDENT STATE
     (1878-1908).
     Bruxelles, 1959.

Afr	29	3	1959	308-9	H. Wakelin Coxill
Af St	18	3	1959	152	C. M. Doke
EHR	75	295	1960	368-9	George Shepperson
RLJ	--	26	1959	72-4	Robert Rotberg

480 Slade, Ruth M.
     KING LEOPOLD'S CONGO; ASPECTS OF THE DEVELOPMENT OF RACE RELA-
     TIONS IN THE CONGO INDEPENDENT STATE.
     London, New York, Oxford University Press, 1962.

Afr	32	4	1962	408-9	A. Roeykens
Af Af	61	245	1962	355	-----
AHR	68	2	1962/63	456-7	David E. Gardinier
Hist	48	163	1963	254	A. J. Hanna
JAH	4	1	1963	140-2	Roger Anstey

481 Smith, Michael Garfield
     GOVERNMENT IN ZAZZAU, 1800-1950.
     London, New York, published for the International African In-
     stitute by the Oxford University Press, 1960.

Afr	31	1	1961	85-6	L. P. Mair
Af Af	61	244	1962	262	Iain Gunn
BSOAS	24	2	1961	404	D. W. A.
JAH	2	2	1961	330-2	A. D. H. Bivar
JMAS	8	1	1970	115-22	Kenneth C. Wylie

482 Smith, Robert Sydney
     KINGDOMS OF THE YORUBA.
     London, Methuen, 1969.

Spence, John Edward

(Smith, Robert Sydney)

Afr	40	1	1970	84	J. D. Y. Peel
Af Af	69	274	1970	79	A. Bolaji Akinyemi
Af SR	--	9	1970	704-5	Ian Henderson
Af St	30	2	1971	161-5	M. D. W. Jeffreys
BSOAS	35	1	1972	211	D. H. Jones
JAH	11	1	1970	162	Colin Newbury

483 Sorrenson, M. P. K.
ORIGINS OF EUROPEAN SETTLEMENT IN KENYA.
Nairobi, Oxford University Press, 1968.

Af Af	69	274	1970	79-81	G. H. Mungeam
AHR	75	5	1969/70	1503-4	Margaret L. Bates
JAH	10	3	1969	511-2	Roland Oliver
JMAS	9	3	1971	487-90	Maina Kagombe

484 Spear, Thomas Turner
ZWANGENDABA'S NGONI 1821-1890. A POLITICAL AND SOCIAL HISTORY
OF A MIGRATION.
Madison University of Wisconsin, African Studies Program,
Occasional Paper 4, 1972.

Afr	44	1	1974	95	J. A. Barnes
IJAHS	6	3	1973	530-1	Gerhard Liesegang

485 Spence, John Edward
LESOTHO: THE POLITICS OF DEPENDENCE.
London, New York, published for the Institute of Race Relations
by Oxford University Press, 1968.

Afr	39	4	1969	422-4	Hugh Ashton
Af Af	67	269	1968	379	G. G. J.
Race	10	1	1968/69	124-5	Christopher R. Hill

486 Spence, John Edward
REPUBLIC UNDER PRESSURE; A STUDY OF SOUTH AFRICAN FOREIGN
POLICY.
London, New York, Oxford University Press, 1965.

Af Af	65	258	1966	101-2	N. E. Mustoe
JMAS	4	1	1966	118	B. Vulindlela Mtshali
Race	7	2	1965/66	207-8	Christopher R. Hill

Stahl, Kathleen Mary

487   Stahl, Kathleen Mary
      HISTORY OF THE CHAGGA PEOPLE OF KILIMANJARO.
      London, Mouton, 1964.

AHR	70	3	1964/65	880	Norman R. Bennett
BSOAS	28	2	1965	436-7	P. H. Gulliver
EHR	81	319	1966	439-40	George Shepperson
JAH	5	3	1964	462-4	Roland Oliver

488   Stamp, Laurence Dudley
      AFRICA; A STUDY IN TROPICAL DEVELOPMENT.
      New York, Wiley, 1953.
      New York, Wiley, 1964 (2d ed.).

      AFRICA, A STUDY IN TROPICAL DEVELOPMENT, BY SIR L. DUDLEY
      STAMP AND W. T. W. MORGAN. 3RD ED.
      New York, Wiley, 1972.

Afr	35	4	1965	446	R. Mansell Prothero
JMAS	11	1	1973	158-9	Gerald L. Karr, Diana
					Conyers

489   Stenning, Derrick J.
      SAVANNAH NOMADS; A STUDY OF THE WODAABE PASTORAL FULANI OF
      WESTERN BORNU PROVINCE, NORTHERN REGION, NIGERIA. WITH A
      FOREWORD BY DARYLL FORDE.
      London, published for the International African Institute by
      the Oxford University Press, 1959.

Afr	30	2	1960	193-5	A. H. M. Kirk-Greene
Af Af	59	234	1960	66-7	D. L. Robinson
Af St	20	4	1961	241-2	Basil L. Sansom
BSOAS	23	1	1960	192-3	D. W. Arnott
JAH	1	1	1960	182-3	P. F. Lacroix

490   Stokes, Eric
      THE ZAMBESIAN PAST; STUDIES IN CENTRAL AFRICAN HISTORY, EDITED
      BY ERIC STOKES AND RICHARD BROWN.
      Manchester, Manchester U.P., 1966.

Afr	37	2	1967	230-1	J. Forbes Munro
Af St	28	1	1969	61-3	Noam J. Pines
AHR	73	3	1967/68	873-5	Robert O. Collins
BSOAS	30	2	1967	454-5	Richard Gray
EHR	83	327	1968	410-1	Henry S. Wilson

Suret-Canale, Jean

(Stokes, Eric)

Hist	53	178	1968	296-7	George Shepperson
JMAS	5	3	1967	430-1	Erving E. Beauregard
Race	8	4	1966/67	428-9	Robert I. Rotberg

491 Summers, Roger
INYANGA; PREHISTORIC SETTLEMENTS IN SOUTHERN RHODESIA. WITH
CONTRIBUTIONS BY H. B. S. COOKE AND OTHERS.
Cambridge, published for the Inyanga Research Fund at the University Press, 1958.

JAH	1	1	1960	151-3	Gervase Mathew

492 Summers, Roger
ZIMBABWE, A RHODESIAN MYSTERY.
Johannesburg, New York, Nelson, 1963.

Afr	36	1	1966	101-3	D. P. Abraham
Af St	23	2	1964	102-3	M. D. W. Jeffreys

493 Sundkler, Bengt Gustaf Malcolm
BANTU PROPHETS IN SOUTH AFRICA.
London, Lutterworth Press, 1948.
London, New York, published for the International African Institute by the Oxford University Press, 1961.

Afr	19	3	1949	248-9	A. I. Richards
Afr	32	2	1962	184-5	Katesa Schlosser
Af Af	48	191	1949	167-8	Max Gluckman
Af Af	65	258	1966	95-6	Laura Longmore
Race	3	2	1961/62	89-90	Ambrose Reeves
Race	6	4	1964/65	342-3	George Bennett
RLJ	--	33	1963	82-94	George Shepperson

494 Suret-Canale, Jean
AFRIQUE NOIRE, OCCIDENTALE ET CENTRALE. PRÉF. DE JEAN DRESCH.
VOL. 1. GÉOGRAPHIE-CIVILISATIONS-HISTOIRE.
VOL. 2. L'ÈRE COLONIALE (1900-1945).
VOL. 3. DE LA COLONISATION AUX INDEPENDANCES (1945-1960).
        CRISE DU SYSTÈME COLONIAL ET CAPITALISME MONOPOLISTE
        D'ÉTAT.
Paris, Éditions sociales, 1958- .

FRENCH COLONIALISM IN TROPICAL AFRICA, 1900-1945. TRANSLATED
FROM THE FRENCH BY TILL GOTTHEIMER.

Swinfen, D. B.

    (Suret-Canale, Jean)
    London, C. Hurst, 1971.
    New York, Pica Press, 1971.

    <u>Vol. 2; Eng. translation</u>

Af Af	71	285	1972	448-51	R. W. Johnson
AHR	80	3	1975	700-1	David E. Gardinier
JAH	13	3	1972	523-4	John D. Hargreaves

    <u>Vol. 3</u>

JAH	15	1	1974	163-4	R. W. Johnson

495   Swinfen, D. B.
      IMPERIAL CONTROL OF COLONIAL LEGISLATION, 1813-1865: A STUDY
      OF BRITISH POLICY TOWARDS COLONIAL LEGISLATIVE POWERS.
      Oxford, Clarendon Press, 1970.

EHR	88	346	1973	201-2	Trevor R. Reese
HJ	15	3	1972	562-9	Ged Martin
Hist	57	190	1972	290	A. H. Will
JAH	13	1	1972	159-60	H. F. Morris

496   Tamrat, Taddesse
      CHURCH AND STATE IN ETHIOPIA, 1270-1527.
      Oxford, Clarendon Press, 1972.

Afr	44	4	1974	427-8	Hector Blackhurst
AHR	80	1	1975	154-5	Robert O. Collins
BSOAS	37	2	1974	456-8	Enrico Cerulli
IJAHS	7	1	1974	129-30	Gildas Nicolas
JAH	15	1	1974	137-40	C. F. Beckingham
JMAS	13	2	1975	361-6	William A. Shack

497   Tamuno, Tekena N.
      THE EVOLUTION OF THE NIGERIAN STATE; THE SOUTHERN PHASE,
      1898-1914.
      London, Longman, 1972.
      New York, Humanities Press, 1972.

Af Af	72	289	1973	455-6	A. H. M. Kirk-Greene
AHR	78	5	1973	1507-8	L. Gray Cowan
BSOAS	36	3	1973	723	David Craig Dorward
JAH	14	3	1973	512-4	John D. Hargreaves
JMAS	11	3	1973	487-9	Samuel O. Okafor

498 Tamuno, Tekena N.
NIGERIA AND ELECTIVE REPRESENTATION, 1923-1947.
London, Ibadan, Heinemann, 1966.

JAH   8   2   1967   366-7   D. H. Jones

499 Taylor, John Vernon
THE GROWTH OF THE CHURCH IN BUGANDA; AN ATTEMPT AT UNDERSTAND-
ING.
London, SCM Press, 1958.

Afr   29   3   1959   313   H. Wakelin Coxill
JAH   1   1   1960   163-6   Roland Oliver

500 Temperley, Howard
BRITISH ANTISLAVERY, 1833-1870.
Columbia, S. C., University of South Carolina Press, 1972.
London, Longman, 1972.

JAH   14   1   1973   156-7   Roger Anstey

501 Temu, A. J.
BRITISH PROTESTANT MISSIONS.
London, Longman, 1972.

Afr   44   2   1974   208-9   F. B. Welbourn
Af Af   74   294   1975   117-8   C. S. Nicholls
BSOAS   37   2   1974   534   Richard Gray
JAH   14   3   1973   520-1   Ian Linden

502 Theobald, Alan Buchan
THE MAHDĪYA; A HISTORY OF THE ANGLO-EGYPTIAN SUDAN, 1881-1899.
London, New York, Longmans, Green, 1951.

Afr   22   4   1952   385-7   R. G. Lienhardt
Af Af   50   201   1951   343-4   Stewart Symes

503 Thompson, Leonard Monteath
POLITICS IN THE REPUBLIC OF SOUTH AFRICA.
Boston, Little, Brown, 1966.

Race   8   2   1966/67   198-200   J. E. Spence

Thompson, Leonard Monteath

504   Thompson, Leonard Monteath
      THE UNIFICATION OF SOUTH AFRICA, 1902-1910.
      Oxford, Clarendon Press, 1960.

Af Af	59	237	1960	338-9	Nelson Mustoe
AHR	66	1	1960/61	108-9	Richard H. Wilde
EHR	76	299	1961	341-2	A. F. McC. Madden
HJ	5	1	1962	102-4	Eric A. Walker
Hist	45	155	1960	287-8	George Bennett
JAH	2	2	1961	337-9	J. D. Fage
Race	2	1	1960/61	71	C. E. Carrington

505   Thompson, Virginia McLean
      DJIBOUTI AND THE HORN OF AFRICA, BY VIRGINIA THOMPSON AND
      RICHARD ADLOFF.
      Stanford, Stanford University Press, 1968.

Af Af	68	272	1969	273-4	Christopher Clapham
Af HS	2	2	1969	373-5	A. A. Castagno
Af St	29	2	1970	146-7	Noam J. Pines
BSOAS	32	3	1969	660-1	I. M. Lewis
JAH	10	4	1969	688-9	V. Luling
JMAS	7	4	1969	760-1	Yousuf Duhul

506   Thompson, Virginia McLean
      FRENCH WEST AFRICA, BY VIRGINIA THOMPSON AND RICHARD ADLOFF.
      Stanford, Stanford University Press, 1957.

Afr	29	1	1959	98	Hubert Deschamps
JAH	1	1	1960	184-5	P. Alexandre

507   Thompson, Virginia McLean
      THE MALAGASY REPUBLIC: MADAGASCAR TODAY, BY VIRGINIA THOMPSON
      AND RICHARD ADLOFF.
      Stanford, Stanford University Press, 1965.

Afr	37	2	1967	231-2	Hubert Deschamps
Af Af	66	264	1967	275-7	John Syson
AHR	72	1	1966/67	257-8	Norman R. Bennett

508   Thompson, Willard Scott
      GHANA'S FOREIGN POLICY, 1957-1966; DIPLOMACY, IDEOLOGY, AND
      THE NEW STATE.
      Princeton, Princeton University Press, 1969.

Trimingham, John Spencer

(Thompson, Willard Scott)
Af Af	70	279	1971	185-6	Richard Rathbone
Af HS	3	1	1970	220-1	John E. Flint
Af StR	14	1	1971	163-5	B. David Meyers
JMAS	8	1	1970	156-9	Jitendra Mohan

509   Thuku, Harry
HARRY THUKU; AN AUTOBIOGRAPHY. WITH ASSISTANCE FROM KENNETH KING.
Nairobi, Oxford University Press, 1970.

Af Af	72	288	1973	343-4	Godfrey Muriuki
IJAHS	6	1	1973	175-6	R. Mugo-Gatheru
JAH	12	4	1971	677	Frank Furedi
JMAS	9	2	1971	335-5	Roger Van Zwanenberg

510   Tordoff, William
ASHANTI UNDER THE PREMPEHS, 1888-1935.
London, Oxford University Press, 1965.

Afr	37	4	1967	489-90	Kwame Arhin
AHR	72	1	1966/67	253-4	Arthur N. Cook
EHR	82	323	1967	434	John D. Hargreaves
Hist	51	173	1966	391-2	D. H. Jones

511   Touval, Saadia
SOMALI NATIONALISM; INTERNATIONAL POLITICS AND THE DRIVE FOR UNITY IN THE HORN OF AFRICA.
Cambridge, Harvard University Press, 1963.

| JMAS | 2 | 1 | 1964 | 130-2 | Hassan A. Mirreh |

512   Trimingham, John Spencer
A HISTORY OF ISLAM IN WEST AFRICA.
London, New York, published for the University of Glasgow by the Oxford University Press, 1962.

Af Af	61	245	1962	354	-----
AHR	68	2	1962/63	533	Nevill Barbour
BSOAS	26	3	1963	678-9	R. B. Serjeant
Hist	48	164	1963	411-2	J. D. Fage
JMAS	1	1	1963	91-7	Thomas Hodgkin

Trimingham, John Spencer

513   Trimingham, John Spencer
        ISLAM IN EAST AFRICA.
        Oxford, Clarendon Press, 1964.

Afr	35	4	1965	445-6	I. M. Lewis
Af Af	64	254	1965	55-6	Geoffrey Parrinder
BSOAS	28	1	1965	201-2	J. N. D. Anderson
JMAS	3	1	1965	147-51	Rev. F. Schildknecht
Race	7	2	1965/66	211-2	Czesław Jeśman

514   Trimingham, John Spencer
        ISLAM IN ETHIOPIA.
        London, New York, Oxford University Press, 1952.

Afr	23	1	1953	75-7	Edward Ullendorff
Af Af	52	206	1953	78-9	E. E. Elder
Af St	11	4	1952	192-3	C. M. Doke
BSOAS	16	2	1954	414-5	Edward Ullendorff

515   Trimingham, John Spencer
        ISLAM IN THE SUDAN.
        London, New York, Oxford University Press, 1949.

Afr	20	1	1950	82-4	Richard Hill
Af Af	48	193	1949	333	Stewart Symes
Af St	9	3	1950	150	C. M. Doke
BSOAS	13	3	1949/51	779-80	R. B. Serjeant

516   Ullendorff, Edward
        THE ETHIOPIANS; AN INTRODUCTION TO COUNTRY AND PEOPLE.
        London, New York, Oxford University Press, 1960.

Afr	30	3	1960	296	G. W. B. Huntingford
Af Af	60	240	1961	450-1	-----
Af Af	64	256	1965	238	-----
AHR	66	1	1960/61	186	Violet Barbour
BSOAS	24	2	1961	393	D. C.
Hist	45	155	1960	281-3	Roland Oliver
JAH	2	1	1961	140-6	Joseph Tubiana
Race	6	4	1964/65	346-7	Czesław Jeśman

517   Universities of East Africa Social Science Conference, 5th,
        Nairobi, 1969.
        WAR AND SOCIETY IN AFRICA; TEN STUDIES, EDITED BY BETHWELL A.
        OGOT.

Vansina, Jan

(Universities of East Africa Social Science Conference)
London, F. Cass, 1972.

Af Af	72	287	1973	203-4	Robert Smith
BSOAS	37	1	1974	284	A. D. Roberts
IJAHS	5	4	1972	707-8	Ralph A. Austen
IJAHS	8	4	1975	702-4	R. F. Morton
JAH	14	2	1973	354	Michael Twaddle

518 Urvoy, Yves François Marie Aimé
HISTOIRE DE L'EMPIRE DU BORNOU.
Paris, Larose, 1949.

| Afr | 20 | 2 | 1950 | 161-3 | H. Richmond Palmer |

519 Van Jaarsveld, Floris Albertus
DIE AFRIKANER EN SY GESKIEDENIS.
Kaapsted, Nasionale Boekhandel, 1959.

| AHR | 66 | 2 | 1960/61 | 496-7 | Colin Rhys Lovell |

520 Van Jaarsveld, Floris Albertus
THE AFRIKANER'S INTERPRETATION OF SOUTH AFRICAN HISTORY.
Cape Town, Simondium Publishers, 1964.

Af Af	64	254	1965	58-9	Marjorie Juta
AHR	70	3	1964/65	786-7	Colin Rhys Lovell
Hist	50	169	1965	266-7	J. L. McCracken
Race	7	2	1965/66	202-5	Edwin S. Munger

521 Van Jaarsveld, Floris Albertus
THE AWAKENING OF AFRIKANER NATIONALISM, 1868-1881. TRANSLATED
BY F. R. METROWICH.
Cape Town, Human and Rousseau, 1961.

AHR	67	4	1961/62	1113-4	Colin Rhys Lovell
EHR	78	309	1963	813-4	Ethel Drus
Hist	47	160	1962	207-8	J. L. McCracken

522 Vansina, Jan
L'ÉVOLUTION DU ROYAUME RWANDA DES ORIGINES À 1900.
Bruxelles, 1962.

Vansina, Jan

(Vansina, Jan)
Afr   32   4   1962   412-3   Marcel d'Hertefelt
JAH   4   2   1963   298-300   Roland Oliver

523   Vansina, Jan
      GESCHIEDENIS VAN DE KUBA, VAN ONGEVEER 1500 TOT 1904.
      Tervuren, Musée Royal de l'Afrique Centrale, Annales, Série
      in-8°, Sciences Humaines, no. 44, 1963.

      Afr   35   2   1965   220   A. A. Trouwborst

524   Vansina, Jan
      KINGDOMS OF THE SAVANNA.
      Madison, University of Wisconsin Press, 1966.

      Af Af   65   261   1966   355-6   J. P. Murray
      AHR   72   2   1966/67   658-9   Robert A. Lystad
      JAH   7   3   1966   514-6   Roland Oliver

525   Vansina, Jan
      ORAL TRADITION; A STUDY IN HISTORICAL METHODOLOGY. TRANSLATED
      BY H. M. WRIGHT.
      Chicago, Aldine Publishing Co., 1965 (c1961).
      London, Routledge and Kegan Paul, 1965.

      DE LA TRADITION ORALE; ESSAI DE MÉTHODE HISTORIQUE.
      Tervuren, Musée Royal de l'Afrique Centrale (Annales, Série
      in-8°, Sciences Humaines, 36), 1961.

      Afr   33   2   1963   157-8   Hubert Deschamps
      BSOAS   29   2   1966   439-40   D. H. Jones
      EHR   82   322   1967   211   J. M. Wallace-Hadrill
      Hist   51   173   1966   386-7   Richard Gray
      JAH   3   3   1962   513-4   C. W. Newbury

526   Vansina, Jan
      THE TIO KINGDOM OF THE MIDDLE CONGO, 1880-1892.
      London, New York, Oxford University Press for the International
      African Institute, 1973.

      Afr   45   3   1975   334-5   John Beattie
      BSOAS   37   2   1974   515-6   Lucy Mair
      JAH   15   3   1974   506-10   Henri Brunschwig

527   Vatcher, Willaim Henry
       WHITE LAAGER; THE RISE OF AFRIKANER NATIONALISM.
       New York, Praeger, 1965.

Af Af	64	257	1965	302-3	Marjorie Juta
AHR	71	2	1965/66	639-40	C. R. Lovell
JMAS	3	4	1965	635-7	P. D. Pillay
Race	7	4	1965/66	424-5	H. J. Simons

528   Verbeken, Auguste
       MSIRI, ROI DU GARENGANZE; L'HOMME ROUGE DU KATANGA.
       Bruxelles, L. Cuypers, 1956.

Afr	27	2	1957	199-200	I. Cunnison

529   Verger, Pierre
       FLUX ET REFLUX DE LA TRAITE DES NÈGRES ENTRE LE GOLFE DE BENIN
       ET BAHIA DE TODOS OS SANTOS, DU XVIIe AU XIXe SIÈCLE.
       Paris, La Haye, Mouton, 1968.

Afr	39	2	1969	194	Hubert Deschamps
Af HS	2	2	1969	347-8	Philip D. Curtin
BSOAS	33	1	1970	232-3	Humphrey J. Fisher
EHR	84	333	1969	806-7	C. R. Boxer
JAH	11	1	1970	151-2	D. Ross

530   Verhaegen, Benoît
       RÉBELLIONS AU CONGO.
       Bruxelles, Centre de Recherche et d'Information Socio-Poli-
       tiques, 1966- .

Vol. 1

Af Af	68	273	1969	370-1	Thomas R. Kanza
AHR	76	4	1971	1201-2	Donald C. Savage
JAH	9	1	1968	180-2	Roger Anstey
JMAS	5	4	1967	579-81	Franz Ansprenger

Vol. 2

Af HS	4	2	1971	398-400	Jacques L. Hymans
JAH	12	1	1971	167	Richard Rathbone
JMAS	10	2	1972	320-2	Catherine Hoskyns

531   Walker, Eric Anderson
       A HISTORY OF SOUTHERN AFRICA. 3RD ED.
       London, New York, Longmans, Green, 1957.

Wallerstein, Immanuel Maurice

(Walker, Eric Anderson)
Af Af   56   225   1957   328   A. G.
EHR   74   290   1959   175-6   A. F. McC. Madden

532   Wallerstein, Immanuel Maurice
      THE ROAD TO INDEPENDENCE: GHANA AND THE IVORY COAST.
      LaHaye, Mouton, 1964.

      JAH   6   3   1965   436-7   Richard Rubens-Rathbone
      Race   7   2   1965/66   202   Claude Welch

533   Walshe, Peter
      THE RISE OF AFRICAN NATIONALISM IN SOUTH AFRICA: THE AFRICAN
      NATIONAL CONGRESS, 1912-1952.
      London, C. Hurst, 1970.

      Af Af   71   283   1972   213-4   Jeffrey Butler
      AHR   80   2   1975   456-7   Harrison M. Wright
      IJAHS   5   2   1972   350-2   Sheridan Johns
      JAH   13   4   1972   699-700   Shula Marks

534   Ward, William Ernest Frank
      A HISTORY OF GHANA.
      London, Allen and Unwin, 1958.
      New York, Praeger, 1963 (c1958).

      A HISTORY OF THE GOLD COAST.
      London, G. Allen and Unwin, 1958.

      Afr   20   3   1950   253-4   J. N. Matson
      Afr   29   4   1959   432   Douglas Jones
      Af Af   48   192   1949   253-4   K. A. B. Jones-Quartey
      AHR   55   1   1949/50   102   Vernon McKay

535   Warhurst, Philip R.
      ANGLO-PORTUGUESE RELATIONS IN SOUTH-CENTRAL AFRICA 1890-1900.
      London, published for the Royal Commonwealth Society by Long-
      mans, 1962.

      EHR   79   310   1964   213-4   Eric Axelson
      Hist   47   161   1962   347   Roland Oliver

536   Webster, James Bertin
       THE AFRICAN CHURCHES AMONG THE YORUBA, 1888-1922.
       Oxford, Clarendon Press, 1964.

       Afr   35   2   1965   223   E. G. Parrinder
       Af Af   65   258   1966   93-4   Geoffrey Parrinder
       BSOAS   28   3   1965   672-3   D. H. Jones
       JAH   6   2   1965   235-7   Max Warren

537   Weinstein, Brian
       ÉBOUÉ.
       New York, Oxford University Press, 1972.

       Af Af   72   288   1973   341   R. W. Johnson
       Af StR   16   2   1973   312-3   James A. Casada
       AHR   80   1   1975   153   Van Mitchell Smith
       IJAHS   5   4   1972   720-2   René Lemarchand
       JAH   14   1   1973   157-9   Jonathan Derrick

538   Welbourn, Frederick Burkewood
       EAST AFRICAN REBELS; A STUDY OF SOME INDEPENDENT CHURCHES.
       London, SCM Press, 1961.

       Afr   31   4   1961   393-4   Robert L. Wishlade
       Af Af   60   241   1961   560   Geoffrey Parrinder
       Hist   47   160   1962   211   A. J. Hanna
       JAH   2   2   1961   340-2   Roland Oliver
       RLJ   --   33   1963   82-94   George Shepperson

539   Welch, Sidney R.
       PORTUGUESE AND DUTCH IN SOUTH AFRICA, 1641-1806.
       Cape Town, Juta, 1951 (i.e., 1952).

       Af St   12   1   1953   31-7   Charles Edward Fuller
       JAH   1   1   1960   55-63   C. R. Boxer

540   Welensky, Sir Roland
       WELENSKY'S 4000 DAYS; THE LIFE AND DEATH OF THE FEDERATION OF
       RHODESIA AND NYASALAND.
       London, Collins, 1964.

       JMAS   3   1   1965   140-3   John Hatch

Welsh, David

541   Welsh, David
      THE ROOTS OF SEGREGATION; NATIVE POLICY IN COLONIAL NATAL,
      1845-1910.
      Cape Town, New York, Oxford University Press, 1971.

IJAHS	6	3	1973	516-9	Leslie Clement Duly
JAH	14	1	1973	151-3	M. D. D. Newitt
JMAS	12	1	1974	137-41	Lawrence Frank

542   WEST AFRICAN CHIEFS; THEIR CHANGING STATUS UNDER COLONIAL RULE
      AND INDEPENDENCE.   EDITED BY MICHAEL CROWDER AND OBARO IKIME.
      TRANSLATIONS FROM THE FRENCH BY BRENDA PACKMAN.
      New York, Africana Pub. Corp., 1970.

Afr	42	2	1972	159-60	Hubert Deschamps
Af HS	4	3	1971	659-68	Martin Klein
EHR	87	342	1972	222-3	John D. Hargreaves
JAH	16	1	1975	149-50	D. H. Jones

543   Wheare, Joan
      THE NIGERIAN LEGISLATIVE COUNCIL.   WITH AN INTROD. BY MARGERY
      PERHAM.
      London, published under the auspices of Nuffield College by
      Faber and Faber, 1950.

Afr	20	3	1950	254-5	L. P. Mair
Af Af	49	196	1950	259-60	Ayo Ogunsheye

544   Wheeler, Douglas L.
      ANGOLA, BY DOUGLAS L. WHEELER AND RENÉ PÉLISSIER.
      London, Pall Mall Press, 1971.
      New York, Praeger, 1971.

Af Af	71	283	1972	212-3	Joseph C. Miller
Af StR	15	1	1972	131-2	Marvin P. Miracle
AHR	77	3	1972	820	F. James Berg
IJAHS	5	1	1972	154-7	Ronald H. Chilcote
JAH	12	4	1971	662-3	David Birmingham
JMAS	11	4	1973	653-5	Thomas H. Henriksen

545   Whiteley, Wilfred Howell
      SWAHILI: THE RISE OF A NATIONAL LANGUAGE.
      London, Methuen, 1969.

Afr	40	3	1970	281-2	A. H. J. Prins
Af HS	3	2	1970	445-7	James L. Brain

(Whiteley, Wilfred Howell)
Af SR	--	9	1970	704-5	Ian Henderson
JAH	11	3	1970	452-3	John Lonsdale
JMAS	8	3	1970	499-501	Anthony Okion Ojigbo

546 Wieschoff, Heinrich Albert
COLONIAL POLICIES IN AFRICA.
Philadelphia, University of Pennsylvania Press, 1944.
Westport, Connecticut, Negro Universities Press, 1972 (c1944).

Afr	15	1	1945	39-40	Charlotte Leubuscher
AHR	50	3	1944/45	590	Harry R. Rudin

547 Wight, Martin
THE DEVELOPMENT OF THE LEGISLATIVE COUNCIL, 1606-1945.
London, Faber and Faber, 1946.

Afr	16	4	1946	275-6	L. P. Mair
Hist	33	119	1948	267-8	W. E. F. Ward

548 Wight, Martin
THE GOLD COAST LEGISLATIVE COUNCIL.
London, pub. under the auspices of Nuffield College by Faber
and Faber, 1947.

Afr	17	4	1947	294-5	L. P. Mair
Af Af	46	185	1947	238-9	Stewart Symes
Hist	33	119	1948	267-8	W. E. F. Ward

549 Wilde, Richard H.
JOSEPH CHAMBERLAIN AND THE SOUTH AFRICAN REPUBLIC, 1895-1899;
A STUDY IN THE FORMULATION OF IMPERIAL POLICY.
Reprinted from the Archives Year Book for South African History, Nineteenth Year, v. 1, 1956.

Hist	44	151	1959	178	Christopher Howard
JAH	4	1	1963	144-5	Ethel Drus

550 Wilks, Ivor
THE NORTHERN FACTOR IN ASHANTI HISTORY.
Legon, Institute of African Studies, University College of
Ghana, 1961.

Wills, Alfred John

(Wilks, Ivor)					
BSOAS	25	2	1962	406-7	J. D. Fage
JAH	3	3	1962	518-9	D. H. Jones

551   Wills, Alfred John
AN INTRODUCTION TO THE HISTORY OF CENTRAL AFRICA.
London, Oxford University Press, 1964.

Af Af	64	255	1965	125	Iain Gunn
Af Af	66	263	1967	176	-----
Af HS	1	1	1968	126-7	L. H. Gann
Af St	24	2	1965	122-4	N. G. Garson
AHR	70	4	1964/65	1114-5	Robert L. Hess
BSOAS	29	2	1966	462	Richard Brown
Hist	50	169	1965	267-8	Anthony Atmore
IJAHS	8	2	1975	304-6	R. E. Schecter
JAH	7	2	1966	349-50	Richard Gray
Race	6	3	1964/65	256	George Shepperson
RLJ	--	37	1965	61-2	Ian Henderson

552   Wilson, Francis
LABOUR IN THE SOUTH AFRICAN GOLD MINES 1911-1969.
Cambridge, University Press, 1972.

Af Af	72	287	1973	214-5	Martin Fransman
Af St	32	3	1973	209-11	D. Hobart Houghton
IJAHS	6	4	1973	658-61	Sheridan Johns
JMAS	12	1	1974	137-41	Lawrence Frank
Race	15	1	1973/74	140-2	Martin Legassick

553   Wilson, Monica (Hunter)
THE OXFORD HISTORY OF SOUTH AFRICA, EDITED BY MONICA WILSON
AND LEONARD THOMPSON.
VOL. 1.   SOUTH AFRICA TO 1870.
VOL. 2.   SOUTH AFRICA 1870-1966.
New York, Oxford University Press, 1969-1971.
Oxford, Clarendon Press, 1969-1971.

Vol. 1

Af Af	69	276	1970	305-7	Nicholas Hyman
Af Af	71	285	1972	444-8	Stanley Trapido
Af HS	3	1	1970	206-7	Leslie Clement Duly
AHR	75	3	1969/70	899-900	Wyn Rees
BSOAS	33	2	1970	435-6	Anthony Atmore
Hist	57	189	1972	153-4	Freda Harcourt

```
(Wilson, Monica (Hunter))
JAH      11  3    1970      435-47    Shula Marks
Race     11  1    1969/70   89-91     Richard Gray

Vol. 2
Af Af    71  285  1972      444-8     Stanley Trapido
Af SR    --  13   1972      228-9     H. J. Simons
Af StR   16  2    1973      291-4     R. Hunt Davis, Jr.
AHR      80  2    1975      456-7     Harrison M. Wright
BSOAS    35  3    1972      678-80    Anthony Atmore
HJ       16  3    1973      616-26    Ronald Hyam
Hist     57  191  1972      473-4     Freda Harcourt
IJAHS    5   4    1972      696-700   Leslie Clement Duly
JAH      13  1    1972      145-50    Martin Legassick
Race     14  1    1972      83-4      Richard Gray
```

554   Wolff, Richard D.
       THE ECONOMICS OF COLONIALISM: BRITAIN AND KENYA, 1870-1930.
       New Haven, Yale University Press, 1974.

```
Afr      45  1    1975      105-6     Lucy Mair
Af Af    74  296  1975      377-9     John Lonsdale
Hist     60  199  1975      256       R. C. Bridges
JAH      15  4    1974      694-6     J. Forbes Munro
Race     16  3    1974/75   337-8     Frank Furedi
```

555   Wraith, Ronald E.
       GUGGISBERG.
       London, Oxford University Press, 1967.

```
Af Af    67  266  1968      69-70     Peter Canham
AHR      73  3    1967/68   873       Philip D. Curtin
BSOAS    30  3    1967      741-2     D. H. Jones
EHR      83  329  1968      878-9     John D. Hargreaves
Hist     53  178  1968      300-1     Christopher Fyfe
JAH      8   3    1967      554-6     J. D. Fage
```

556   Wright, Marcia
       GERMAN MISSIONS IN TANGANYIKA, 1891-1941: LUTHERANS AND
       MORAVIANS IN THE SOUTHERN HIGHLANDS.
       Oxford, Clarendon Press, 1971.

```
Af Af    71  284  1972      346-7     Aylward Shorter
AHR      80  2    1975      451       Robert W. Strayer
IJAHS    5   3    1972      524-6     Per Hassing
JMAS     10  3    1972      495-6     Jake W. Spidle, Jr.
```

Young, Crawford

557   Young, Crawford
       POLITICS IN THE CONGO; DECOLONIZATION AND INDEPENDENCE.
       Princeton, Princeton University Press, 1965.

Afr	37	3	1967	357-8	G. Malengreau
Af Af	65	260	1966	266-7	J. P. M.
Af Af	67	268	1968	253-4	R. W. Johnson
AHR	71	1	1965/66	273	P. D. Curtin
JMAS	4	1	1966	111-5	Colin Legum

558   Yudelman, Montague
       AFRICANS ON THE LAND; ECONOMIC PROBLEMS OF AFRICAN AGRICUL-
       TURAL DEVELOPMENT IN SOUTHERN, CENTRAL, AND EAST AFRICA, WITH
       SPECIAL REFERENCE TO SOUTHERN RHODESIA.
       Cambridge, Harvard University Press, 1964.

Af Af	64	254	1965	45-6	W. V. Blewett
BSOAS	28	2	1965	441-2	P. H. Gulliver
JMAS	2	4	1964	609-13	Selby B. Ngcobo

559   Zolberg, Aristide R.
       CREATING POLITICAL ORDER; THE PARTY-STATES OF WEST AFRICA.
       Chicago, Rand McNally, 1966.

Afr	38	2	1968	210-1	K. W. J. Post
Af Af	69	277	1970	404-5	Margaret L. Bates
JAH	8	3	1967	563-5	Richard Rubens-Rathbone
JMAS	5	2	1967	281-3	William J. Foltz
JMAS	7	1	1969	107-30	Jon Kraus

560   Zolberg, Aristide R.
       ONE-PARTY GOVERNMENT IN THE IVORY COAST.
       Princeton, Princeton University Press, 1964.

Afr	25	3	1965	326-8	S. K. Panter-Brick
Afr	40	2	1970	194	-----
Af Af	63	253	1964	309	-----
Af Af	69	277	1970	404-5	Margaret L. Bates
JAH	5	3	1964	465-8	Kenneth Robinson
JMAS	2	4	1964	594-6	Henry Bienen
Race	6	3	1964/65	253-4	Claude Welch

Author/Title Index

Title or co-author followed by book entry number.

A

A LA RECHERCHE D'UN ÉTAT INDÉ-
PENDANT: 215
ADAMAWA PAST AND PRESENT: 300
Ade Ajayi, J. F., see Ajayi,
J. F. Ade
Adloff, Richard. DJIBOUTI AND
THE HORN OF AFRICA: 505
Adloff, Richard. FRENCH WEST
AFRICA: 506
Adloff, Richard. MALAGASY
REPUBLIC, THE: 507
ADMINISTRATION OF NIGERIA,
1900-1960, THE: 393
AFRICA; A STUDY IN TROPICAL
DEVELOPMENT: 488
AFRICA AND AFRICANS: 73
AFRICA AND THE VICTORIANS: 450
AFRICA IN SEARCH OF DEMOCRACY:
93
AFRICA IN SOCIAL CHANGE: 329
AFRICA IN TIME-PERSPECTIVE: 343
AFRICA: ITS PEOPLES AND THEIR
CULTURE HISTORY: 383
AFRICA SINCE 1875: 224
AFRICA: THE HISTORY OF A
CONTINENT: 139
AFRICA TO 1875: 225
AFRICAN BOURGEOISIE, AN: 309
AFRICAN CHURCHES AMONG THE
YORUBA, 1888-1922, THE: 536
AFRICAN ÉLITE, AN: 201
AFRICAN GENIUS, THE: 140
AFRICAN LAW: 308

AFRICAN LIBERATION MOVEMENTS:
200
AFRICAN NATIONALISM: 477
AFRICAN OPPOSITION IN SOUTH
AFRICA: 170
AFRICAN PATRIOTS, THE: 58
AFRICAN POLICIES OF GABRIEL
HANOTAUX, 1894-1898, THE:
239
AFRICAN POLITICAL PARTIES, AN
INTRODUCTORY GUIDE: 252
AFRICAN POLITICS AND BRITISH
POLICY IN THE GOLD COAST,
1868-1900: 11
AFRICAN SURVEY, AN: 221
AFRICAN TRADERS IN KUMASI: 197
AFRICAN TRIBES AND EUROPEAN
AGENCIES: 257
AFRICAN VOICE IN SOUTHERN
RHODESIA, 1898-1930, THE:
440
AFRICANS, THE: 140
AFRICANS ON THE LAND: 558
AFRICA'S SEARCH FOR IDENTITY:
172
AFRIKANER BOND, THE: 138
AFRIKANER EN SY GESKIEDENIS, DIE:
519
AFRIKANER'S INTERPRETATION OF
SOUTH AFRICAN HISTORY, THE:
520
AFRIQUE; LES CIVILISATIONS NOIRES:
353
AFRIQUE NOIRE, OCCIDENTALE ET
CENTRALE: 494

D

Daget, Jacques. L'EMPIRE PEUL
DU MACINA: 41
DAHOMEAN NARRATIVE: 241
DAHOMEY AND ITS NEIGHBOURS,
1708-1818: 15
DAILY LIFE IN THE KINGDOM OF
THE KONGO: 44
DAMNÉS DE LA TERRE, LES: 168
DANISH SETTLEMENTS IN WEST
AFRICA, 1658-1850: 397
de Azevedo, Carlos, see Azevedo,
Carlos de
DE LA COLONISATION AUX INDE-
PENDANCES (1945-1960), see
AFRIQUE NOIRE, OCCIDENTALE
ET CENTRALE
DE LA TRADITION ORALE: 525
DÉCOLONISATION, 1919-1963, LA:
217
Denny, Alice. AFRICA AND THE
VICTORIANS: 450
DEVELOPMENT OF THE LEGISLATIVE
COUNCIL, 1606-1945, THE:
547
DILEMMAS OF TRUSTEESHIP, THE:
448
DJIBOUTI AND THE HORN OF
AFRICA: 505
Dotson, Lillian O., see Dotson,
Floyd
Duignan, Peter. BURDEN OF
EMPIRE: 192
Duignan, Peter. COLONIALISM IN
AFRICA, 1870-1960: 193
DUTCH SEABORNE EMPIRE, 1600-
1800, THE: 75

E

E. D. MOREL'S HISTORY OF THE
CONGO REFORM MOVEMENT: 373
EARLY KINGDOMS IN MADAGASCAR,
1500-1700: 294
EAST AFRICA: UGANDA, KENYA,
TANGANYIKA, see NATIVE AD-
MINISTRATION IN THE BRITISH
AFRICAN TERRITORIES
EAST AFRICAN CHIEFS: 444

EAST AFRICAN REBELS: 538
ÉBOUÉ: 537
ECONOMIC HISTORY OF ETHIOPIA,
1800-1935: 416
ECONOMIC HISTORY OF WEST AFRICA,
AN: 260
ECONOMICS OF COLONIALISM, THE,
see COLONIALISM IN AFRICA,
1870-1960
ECONOMICS OF COLONIALISM:
BRITAIN AND KENYA, 1870-1930,
THE: 554
EDUCATIONAL DEVELOPMENT IN THE
SUDAN, 1898-1956: 62
EDWARD WILMOT BLYDEN: PAN-NEGRO
PATRIOT 1832-1912: 341
EFFECTS OF ECONOMIC DEVELOPMENT
ON TRADITIONAL POLITICAL
SYSTEMS IN AFRICA SOUTH OF
THE SAHARA, THE: 369
EGBA AND THEIR NEIGHBOURS,
1842-1872, THE: 68
EGYPT IN THE SUDAN, 1820-1881:
249
ELITES OF BAROTSELAND, 1878-1969,
THE: 98
EMIRATES OF NORTHERN NIGERIA,
THE: 254
EMPIRE PEUL DU MACINA, L': 41
EMPIRE TOUCOULEUR, 1848-1897, L':
461
ENGLISH-SPEAKING MISSIONS IN THE
CONGO INDEPENDENT STATE
(1878-1908): 479
ÈRE COLONIALE (1900-1945), L',
see AFRIQUE NOIRE, OCCIDENTALE
ET CENTRALE
ESSAYS IN IMPERIAL GOVERNMENT:
449
ETHIOPIA, A CULTURAL HISTORY: 415
ETHIOPIA; A NEW POLITICAL HISTORY:
212
ETHIOPIA: THE ERA OF THE PRINCES:
2
ETHIOPIA; THE MODERNIZATION OF
AUTOCRACY: 244
ETHIOPIA, THE STUDY OF A POLITY,
1540-1935: 365
ETHIOPIAN PARADOX, THE: 280
ETHIOPIANS, THE: 516
EUROPEAN POLITICS IN SOUTHERN
RHODESIA: 325

Gollnhofer, Otto. BRAZZA ET LA
PRISE DE POSSESSION DU
CONGO: 119

GOVERNMENT AND MISSION EDUCATION
IN NORTHERN NIGERIA, 1900–
1919: 205

GOVERNMENT AND POLITICS IN
TRIBAL SOCIETIES: 464

GOVERNMENT IN ZAZZAU, 1800–1950:
481

GOVERNMENT OF ETHIOPIA, THE:
423

GRAND ILLUSION, A: 144

GREAT BRITAIN AND GERMANY'S LOST
COLONIES, 1914–1919: 333

GREAT BRITAIN AND SOUTH AFRICAN
CONFEDERATION, 1870–1881:
202

GROWTH OF BOER OPPOSITION TO
KRUGER, 1890–1895, THE:
204

GROWTH OF THE CHURCH IN BUGANDA,
THE: 499

GUGGISBERG: 555

H

HAILE SELASSIE: THE CONQUERING
LION, see HAILE SELASSIE I:
THE CONQUERING LION

HAILE SELASSIE I: THE CONQUERING
LION: 377

HARRY THUKU; AN AUTOBIOGRAPHY:
509

Herskovits, Frances S. DAHOMEAN
NARRATIVE: 241

Herskovits, Melville J. CON-
TINUITY AND CHANGE IN
AFRICAN CULTURES: 51

HIGH COMMISSION TERRITORIES:
BASUTOLAND, THE BECHUANALAND
PROTECTORATE AND SWAZILAND,
see NATIVE ADMINISTRATION
IN THE BRITISH AFRICAN TER-
RITORIES

HISTOIRE DE L'AFRIQUE: 121

HISTOIRE DE L'AFRIQUE NOIRE,
D'HIER À DEMAIN: 302

HISTOIRE DE L'AFRIQUE OCCIDENTALE:
391

HISTOIRE DE L'EMPIRE DU BORNOU:
518

HISTOIRE DE LA TRAITE DES NOIRS
DE L'ANTIQUITÉ À NOS JOURS:
147

HISTOIRE DE MADAGASCAR: 148

HISTOIRE DES PEUPLES DE
L'AFRIQUE NOIRE: 122

HISTOIRE DES PEUPLES NOIRS: 6

HISTOIRE DU DAHOMEY: 123

HISTOIRE DU TOGO: 124

HISTORIAN IN TROPICAL AFRICA,
THE: 274

HISTORICAL SURVEY OF THE ORIGINS
AND GROWTH OF MAU MAU: 120

HISTORY AND POLITICS OF COLONIAL-
ISM, 1870–1914, THE, see
COLONIALISM IN AFRICA, 1870–
1960

HISTORY AND POLITICS OF COLONIAL-
ISM, 1914–1960, THE, see
COLONIALISM IN AFRICA, 1870–
1960

HISTORY OF BRITAIN IN AFRICA FROM
THE FIFTEENTH CENTURY TO THE
PRESENT, THE: 238

HISTORY OF BUGANDA, A: 301

HISTORY OF EAST AFRICA, A: 271

HISTORY OF GHANA, A: 534

HISTORY OF ISLAM IN WEST AFRICA,
A: 512

HISTORY OF KENYA'S TRADE UNION
MOVEMENT, TO 1952: 476

HISTORY OF MALINDI, THE: 361

HISTORY OF NATAL, A: 87

HISTORY OF NORTHERN RHODESIA,
EARLY DAYS TO 1953, A: 194

HISTORY OF SIERRA LEONE, A: 183

HISTORY OF SIERRA LEONE, 1400–
1787, A: 307

HISTORY OF SOUTH AFRICA, THE,
see THE OXFORD HISTORY OF
SOUTH AFRICA

HISTORY OF SOUTHERN AFRICA, A:
531

HISTORY OF SOUTHERN RHODESIA, A:
195

HISTORY OF THE AFRICAN PEOPLE, A:
285

HISTORY OF THE ASIANS IN EAST
AFRICA, c. 1886 TO 1945, A:
350

I

J

Q

R

Reviewer Index

Name of reviewer followed by book entry number(s) containing review(s).

A. F. H.: 380
A. G.: 531
A. M.: 395
B. M.: 210
D. C.: 516
D. H. S.: 155
D. W. A.: 481
E. A.: 162
E. M.: 261
F. G. B.: 43
G. F.: 241
G. G. J.: 485
H. V. L. S.: 143
J. P.: 445
J. P. M.: 264, 453, 557
L. L.: 143
P. M. H.: 62
P. S.: 358
R. M.: 139, 414
R. R.: 455
S. S.: 125, 258, 405, 450
S. T.: 125
W. A. G. M.: 164
W. E.: 262

A

Abbott, Sally: 210
Abir, Mordechai: 323
Abraham, D. P.: 492
Abrahams, Roy G.: 32, 208, 270, 472
Adler, S.: 237
Ady, P.: 53

Afigbo, A. E.: 186, 305, 468
Aguda, Oluwadare: 128
Ajayi, J. F. Ade: 28, 151, 233, 425
Akinjogbin, I. A.: 389
Akinyemi, A. Bolaji: 482
Albino, Oliver: 63
Alden, Dauril: 77
Alexandre, Pierre: 108, 137, 506
Allchin, Bridget: 109, 113
Allott, A. N.: 167, 203, 233
Allyn, David E.: 5
Alpers, Edward A.: 36, 228
Alport, E. A.: 74
Amachree, Igolima T. D.: 327
Amamos, Joseph: 163
Amsden, Alice H.: 476
Anderson, J. N. D.: 513
Andrzejewski, B. W.: 245
Anglin, Douglas G.: 84, 281
Ansprenger, Franz: 33, 159, 168, 198, 220, 530
Anstey, Roger T.: 28, 69, 96, 115, 119, 134, 147, 198, 215, 291, 312, 340, 373, 429, 455, 467, 480, 500, 530
Apter, David E.: 127, 299
Apthorpe, R. J.: 162
Ardener, Edwin: 166, 179, 201, 320
Argyle, W. J.: 15
Arhin, Kwame: 184, 510
Arkell, A. J.: 259, 471
Arnold, Percy: 377
Arnott, D. W.: 41, 205, 300, 489

Buxton, Jean: 63

C

Cady, John F.: 90
Canham, Peter H.: 295, 555
Caplan, Gerald L.: 367
Cares, P. B.: 75
Carrington, C. E.: 504
Carter, Gwendolen M.: 200, 421
Casada, James A.: 301, 537
Castagno, A. A.: 34, 505
Caulk, Richard A.: 416
Cawson, Alan: 411
Cecil, Charles O.: 3, 275
Cerulli, Enrico: 324, 496
Chadwick, Owen: 453
Chambers, Robert: 399
Charles, Eunice A.: 180
Charton, Nancy: 347
Chilcote, Ronald H.: 544
Chittick, Neville: 113
Clapham, Christopher: 100, 505
Clark, M. L.: 110, 209
Cline, Catherine Ann: 467
Cobban, A.: 149
Cohen, Abner: 160, 265
Cohen, David William: 208, 243
Cohen, Robin: 436
Cohen, William B.: 90, 129
Collard, Claude A.: 231, 283
Collins, Robert O.: 1, 17, 63,
    82, 192, 315, 334, 404, 409,
    490, 496
Colson, E.: 165
Conyers, Diana: 488
Cook, Arthur N.: 185, 194, 234,
    510
Cook, M. A.: 293
Cooke, C. M.: 158
Cooke, James J.: 188
Copans, Jean: 131
Cope, R. L.: 343
Cottingham, Clement: 54, 131
Cowan, L. Gray: 126, 247, 305,
    400, 435, 456, 497
Coxill, H. Wakelin: 479, 499
Craig, George: 230
Cross, Malcolm: 431
Crowder, Michael: 150, 180, 394

Crowfoot, J. W.: 27, 258
Cruise O'Brien, Donal: 44, 303
Cruise O'Brien, Rita: 112
Crummey, Donald: 2, 458
Cumming, Duncan C.: 72, 346
Cunnison, Ian: 258, 464, 470,
    528
Curry, George: 229
Curtin, Philip D.: 14, 25, 50,
    260, 286, 335, 346, 383, 424,
    433, 451, 459, 529, 555, 557

D

Dachs, A. J.: 95
Dale, Richard: 71, 200, 333
Dammann, E.: 43
Davenport, T. R. H.: 86, 95, 156,
    171, 204, 422
Davidson, Basil: 125, 404
Davidson, John: 425
Davies, J. D.: 453
Davies, K. G.: 78, 185
Davis, Lenwood G.: 8
Davis, R. Hunt, Jr.: 475, 553
Dawn, C. Ernest: 249
Day, John: 477
Dean, David: 477
Deighton, H. S.: 207, 259
de Kiewiet, C. W.: 48, 267, 363
Denoon, Donald: 350, 440, 462
Derrick, Jonathan: 38, 407, 537
Deschamps, Hubert: 8, 28, 73,
    112, 119, 122, 124, 127, 129,
    134, 173, 235, 238, 288, 294,
    338, 343, 351, 376, 443, 451,
    506, 507, 525, 529, 542
Dickson, Alec: 182, 248
Diffie, Bailey W.: 154
Diké, K. O.: 268
Dipoko, Mbella Sonne: 338, 376
Doke, C. M.: 479, 514, 515
Dorward, David Craig: 31, 126,
    247, 435, 497
Douglas, Mary: 23
Downum, Garland: 294
Doxey, G. V.: 309
Doxey, Margaret: 48
Driver, Jonty: 418
Drus, Ethel: 355, 521, 549

Mangat, J. S.: 152, 266
Maquet, Jacques: 243, 334
Marcus, Harold G.: 2, 115, 245, 324
Markham, J. G.: 292
Markov, Walter: 217, 351, 448
Marks, Shula: 58, 67, 87, 145, 202, 250, 267, 285, 339, 375, 381, 409, 418, 533, 553
Martin, Eveline: 151
Martin, Ged: 103, 495
Martin, Jane: 327
Martin, Phyllis: 439
Mason, Philip: 135, 140, 196, 247
Mathew, Gervase: 74, 491
Matson, J. N.: 534
Mauny, R.: 121, 142, 313, 321, 343
Mayer, A. C.: 152
Mayer, Philip: 49
Meillassoux, C.: 203
Mellini, Peter: 116
Messing, Simon D.: 244
Metcalfe, G. E.: 103
Meyerowitz, Eva L. R.: 10
Meyers, B. David: 508
Middleton, John: 120, 190, 206, 250, 314, 332
Miers, Suzanne: 118, 373, 443
Miles, John: 130
Millar-Craig, H.: 297
Miller, Joseph C.: 446, 544
Minchinton, W. E.: 134
Miracle, Marvin P.: 544
Mirreh, Hassan A.: 511
Mitchison, Naomi: 40
Mohan, Jitendra: 399, 401, 408, 411, 508
Morgan, E. Philip: 232
Morrell, W. P.: 89
Morris, H. F.: 290, 308, 495
Morris, H. S.: 152, 350
Mortimer, Robert A.: 54
Morton, R. F.: 517
Motani, Nizar A.: 83, 213, 224
Moyse-Bartlett, H.: 405
Mtshali, B. Vulindlela: 486
Mudenge, S. I.: 462
Mueller, Susanne D.: 199
Muffett, D. J. M.: 247

Mugo-Gatheru, R.: 509
Mungeam, G. H.: 483
Munger, Edwin S.: 520
Munro, J. Forbes: 490, 554
Muriuki, Godfrey: 509
Murray, J. P.: 23, 524
Mustoe, Nelson E.: 25, 58, 220, 423, 486, 504
Muth, E. L.: 227

N

Nadel, S. F.: 423
Nafziger, E. Wayne: 296
Nanza, T. R.: 198
Neame, Sylvia: 287
Newbury, Colin W.: 12, 90, 123, 127, 135, 234, 235, 254, 300, 341, 397, 450, 463, 465, 482, 525
Newitt, M. D. D.: 181, 446, 541
Ngcobo, Selby B.: 558
Nicholls, B. M.: 87
Nicholls, C. S.: 361, 501
Nicolas, Gildas: 496
Niven, Rex: 247
Nixon, Charles R.: 434, 478
Nkemdirim, Bernard: 435
Noak, H.: 57
Northrup, David: 186, 269

O

Obichere, Boniface I.: 130
O'Connor, E.: 285
Offiong, Daniel A.: 407
Ofoegbu, Mazi Ray: 172
Ogunsheye, Ayo: 543
Ogutu, Matthias A.: 208
Ojigbo, Anthony Okion: 545
Okafor, Samuel O.: 7, 497
Okuma, Thomas: 107
Oliver, Caroline: 454
Oliver, Roland A.: 32, 36, 37, 76, 88, 97, 148, 155, 161, 181, 190, 203, 206, 229, 256, 272, 333, 334, 335, 372, 417, 441, 447, 472, 483, 487, 499, 516, 522, 524, 535, 538